DOREEN KERRY

Pathway to the Moon

Looking back on a
life of daydreaming
with the stars

DOREEN KERRY

Pathway to the Moon

Looking back on a
life of daydreaming
with the stars

MEREO
Cirencester

Mereo Books

1A The Wool Market Dyer Street Cirencester Gloucestershire GL7 2PR
An imprint of Memoirs Publishing www.mereobooks.com

Pathway to the Moon: 978-1-86151-864-4

First published in Great Britain in 2017
by Mereo Books, an imprint of Memoirs Publishing

The address for Memoirs Publishing Group Limited can be found at
www.memoirspublishing.com

The Memoirs Publishing Group Ltd Reg. No. 7834348

The Memoirs Publishing Group supports both The Forest Stewardship Council® (FSC®) and the PEFC® leading international forest-certification organisations. Our books carrying both the FSC label and the PEFC® and are printed on FSC®-certified paper. FSC® is the only forest-certification scheme supported by the leading environmental organisations including Greenpeace. Our paper procurement policy can be found at www.memoirspublishing.com/environment

Typeset in 12/18pt Century Schoolbook
by Wiltshire Associates Publisher Services Ltd. Printed and bound in Great Britain by Printondemand-Worldwide, Peterborough PE2 6XD

This book is dedicated to my husband (1958-2012),
who has left a footprint in my heart that can
never be erased, and to one special lady who I was
proud to call Mum (1934-2014).

CONTENTS

PREFACE

If it is true that mighty oaks from little acorns grow, then this little acorn came from the strongest trees in the whole forestry world - my parents. Throughout life they were both my strength and my shield, and without them l do not think I could have stood the test of time.

Writing this, my first book, has put me on the path to destiny. It has helped to pull me out of the doldrums – an apt expression, in fact, since I have set out to take my readers on a voyage of discovery whilst I have been grieving (in the wrong order). But then again, why be normal?

This is a light-hearted look at how my life was before it was all "Gone with the Wind" – ironic, since it involved me hopping in and out of my own customised time machine and flitting from one film set to another in an imaginary world at the time when I had all life's treasures in the palm of my hand.

I cannot change what happened and my grief can never be erased, but in spite of having lost the love of my life, and others that were dear to me, I refuse to let the world make me hard.

Have a look inside and laugh with me if you will, as

I have done in the face of adversity. Whilst I have had many a philosophical moan along the way I am seeking unbiased opinions that I have not gone absolutely potty.

Whether you are a film buff or not, I am confident there will be a little bit of you tucked nicely away among the words in the paragraphs which are set not to dampen but to uplift the spirit as I raise a glass to the man to whom this book is dedicated and who never got to know the half of what he married. Indeed he had a lucky escape.

ACKNOWLEDGMENTS

The references to films in this book are based on the fact that I have at some time watched them all and therefore feel justified that I can cite them in this way, in no particular order.

Gone with the Wind (1939)

The Time Machine (1960)

Whatever Happened to Baby Jane? (1962)

Dead Men Don't Wear Plaid (1982)

The Road to Bali (1952)

Scrooge (1951)

The Great St Trinian's Train Robbery (1966)

Psycho (1960)

The Man in the Iron Mask (1968)

Shirley Valentine (1989)

Alice's Adventures in Wonderland (written 1865)

Alice Through the Looking Glass (written 1891)

Arsenic and Old Lace (1944)

Murder on the Orient Express (1974)

Zulu (1964)

Enigma (2001)

You've Got Mail (1998)

The Diary of Anne Frank (1959)

Saving Private Ryan (1998)

Pearl Harbour (2001)

Big (1988)

Albert RN (1953)

Reach for the Sky (1956)

Wizard of Oz (1939)

Home Alone (1990)

*Charlie and the
Chocolate Factory (2005)*

Casablanca (1942)

Now Voyager (1942)

Mr Skeffington (1944)

The Old Maid (1939)

The Letter (1940)

Dark Victory (1939)

Gettysburg (1993)

Glory (1989)

Bhowani Junction (1956)

Waterloo Bridge (1940)

The Railway Children (1970)

*By the Light of the Silvery
Moon (1953)*

On Moonlight Bay (1951)

Brief Encounter (1945)

Titanic (1997)

Patch Adams (1998)

Houseboat (1958)

Father Goose (1964)

Pinocchio (1940)

The Light in the Piazza (1962)

Random Harvest (1942)

The Roman Spring of Mrs Stone (1961)

Raintree County (1957)

INTRODUCTION

The beauty of a woman is not in the clothes she wears, the figure she carries or the way she combs her hair.

The beauty of a woman must be seen in her eyes, because that is the doorway to her heart, the place where love resides.

The beauty of a woman is not in a facial mole, but the true beauty of a woman is reflected in her soul.

It is the caring that she lovingly gives, the passion that she shows, and the beauty of a woman with passing years only grows. –

Audrey Hepburn, 1929-1993

Many a time I have looked at the life of a movie star and wanted that glitz and glamour for myself. Oh to have been a part of MGM – the studio that had more stars than there were in heaven! A world where hour-glass figures were the norm, with clothes that caressed every voluptuous curve and where the 'peek-a-boo' hair style made famous by Veronica Lake was emulated most famously by Lauren Bacall and the platinum Hollywood blondes who personified a sheer sophistication that is difficult to match these days.

I have never been on a film set, but I should hope that if the opportunity ever arose, I could sweet-talk the camera crew into letting me go behind the scenes so I could get in on the action. Since this is very unlikely, I hope the creation of this book will allow me to put myself in the driving seat so that I can magically transport myself and my readers back through the golden age of the cinema, television and those classic movies.

There may be times when I become over-enthusiastic with ideas and go into overdrive, as it were, so permission is granted to whack on the literary handbrake at any point in time and price it up for the next car boot sale!

H G Wells was not the only one who had a time machine; so do I, except that mine is in my head. Where I choose to end up and with whom is anyone's guess. In the world of entertainment, anything is possible.

I seek to recruit an audience that shares my great passion for such dreams, but if, like the dumb actress working towards a part in a movie who has slept with the writer instead of the producer, then please exit the stage right now, as you just won't get me any more than I get you.

If, on the other hand, like me (and my old mate Dorothy), you are forever seeking lemon drops way above the chimney tops, then join me on a magical ride across the rainbow as I strive to cut my journalistic teeth here and on the 'net.'

My illusions of grandeur on the silver screen or when floating around Tinseltown in some disguise or another may warrant your forgiveness, but for all my playfulness and creative ingenuity there will be a serious message to be found here, if you care to read between the lines.

So pull up a comfortable armchair with matching footstool, fasten your seat belt and join me on a hopefully not too bumpy ride as we orbit through Universal Studios and beyond, in a totally ridiculous way.

January 2018

TIME ON MY HANDS

As the keen scrap-booker from my youth is left behind, my creative journey is set to begin, and armed with plenty of imagination, nostalgia, humour and inspiration, I set forth. I cannot promise this book will be a work of art, but hopefully it will entertain the mind of anyone who happens to stumble upon it by chance.

Consider it more a memoir than an autobiography – an intimate insight into my feelings and emotions as not portrayed anywhere else; times in my life that cannot be rewritten; history in the making.

Who knows, maybe some famous publisher will make a fortunate discovery of me on ebay whilst looking for reading material that is entirely different and I will become someone's serendipitous find. No doubt the words 'sex', 'money' or 'free' in the search bar would guarantee far more interest than the random title I have created here today. Yet it bothers me not, as once I get into my imaginary time machine (parked up in the corner of my living room), I shall not be deterred.

The gearbox has a four-speed manual transmission – an advanced version of Mr Wells' iconic time machine in the story by the same name. As I pull on the gear stick that comes horizontally out of the dashboard, much like that of my sister's old Citroen Dyane in the early 80s, I am looking forward to my first adventure. Having made a column change through from first to fourth gear, I take off in a most disorderly fashion. As I watch, the Yankee candle in the corner of the room melts in a matter of seconds and a small snail scampers across my laminate flooring. I am on my way.

Having shot through the open door of my conservatory and being now in orbit, I can see the sun and moon bouncing back and forth in the sky like ping-pong balls, competing with small spherical capsules of rice paper filled with sherbet – edible flying saucers, no less – and a mannequin in a store window below marks the generations by the raising of hemlines and the changing of accessories.

Then, right before my eyes, the dummy assumes the appearance of Ebenezer Scrooge. He smirks, and over the noise of the engine he acts out his best sign language to tell me that I am a little behind the times

– he has already travelled to Christmases past, present and future. So he may have been one step ahead of me in the transport business, I am thinking, but I am not about to let him steal my thunder!

It has been said that 'old age is like flying through a storm and once you're aboard there's nothing you can do about it' (Golda Meir), but I remain confident that whilst I am still able to understand what I am doing, whilst I am still able to retain that train of thought, whilst I am still able to weigh up the pros and cons of making this journey and others, and whilst I am still in a position to be able to communicate to the world the fun I have had, then I can rest assured that I still have full mental capacity to carry out the task – and that whilst I may be getting on a little, I am not dead and buried quite yet!

After observing events in superfast motion from inside my velvet-cushioned contraption, I decide to put on the handbrake and step outside. I have travelled back to the 1960s, where I am once more a child. I am petrified at some of the events that have flashed past me like holograms, such as the shooting of Senator Robert F Kennedy, the slaying of Martin Luther King, India's worst famine in 20 years and the horrific events of the Vietnamese war. I had heard about them on the news, but now it is real life and very daunting. I am thinking that this is no place for me.

As I proceed to go back and forth in time in a somewhat random fashion while hovering around the same era, I stop off briefly at a motel. All this time-travelling is making me hot and I am in desperate need of a shower. The owner looks a bit of a psycho to me. He tells me his name is Norman. Asking me to sign in, his voice is quite sinister. It bears a chilling resemblance to that of a woman who calls down to him from the attic. He explains it is his mother, Mrs Bates. I had caught a glimpse of her in the window as I pulled up. I could have sworn she was sitting in a rocking chair, or perhaps it was an original yet-to-be-patented gaming chair, but from where I was standing she definitely looked like death warmed up.

Then I heard the dreadful screeching of violins and knew this was my cue to either get out of there fast or be stabbed to death in the shower later. Hmm... tough decision or what?

I need to move things on a little, so, having uploaded Google Earth on my state of the art Intel computer, it a case of ground control to Major Tom. As I observe the sun and moon traversing the sky yet again, I am hovering around in a most peculiar way and the stars look very different today.

Whilst Beatlemania is going on around the country and hippies are walking around chanting about love and peace, I have somehow progressed to 1969 and find myself in the foyer of the Odeon picture house in Muswell Hill, North London. Just like my Hollywood idols I have longed to be in the spotlight, but I am not ready to face too big an audience just yet. Having put myself in the limelight at Saturday morning pictures, it is indeed a starting point – even if only in front of a bunch of school kids.

Enter me – the usherette. The doors have opened, and as I insist on showing the fresh-faced youngsters to their seats it is free viewing for me, and I wait patiently on the sidelines to serve popcorn, ice cream and other refreshments from the vendor tray that has been strategically placed around my neck during the intermission.

Although I'm not one who normally confesses to be stunningly beautiful or impeccably poised, as I stand there in my little black and white outfit resembling that of a French maid, I feel particularly attractive and important. The outfit is a far cry from my usual work attire, which does little for my self-esteem. The high heels in place of 'sensible' shoes give me the height I have always craved, and whilst they may not give me the seductive sway of Marilyn Monroe with her mesmerising wiggles, you can't blame me for wanting a little help to be able to see and be seen at least one day of the week.

I check my little fob watch constantly, hoping that time will not race by too quickly and that unlike Cinderella, I will not have to leave the ball before all showings have ended, as I am having a ball on my own! What power I have with my torch as I take delight in policing the theatre, shining it across all those loved-up teeny boppers in the back rows trying to steal a kiss while the lights are out. The green-eyed monster is rearing its ugly head.

The Martini advert that popped up frequently during the screenings speaks of having it 'any time, any place, anywhere' but if they thought they could embrace that attitude in my theatre then they had another think coming.

Old Mother Riley is the key feature this morning. So naïve am I that I have not cottoned on that 'mother' is a man in drag; all credit to Arthur Lucan, who is playing the part admirably, even convincingly, as an Irish washerwoman whose antics are making the audience roar with laughter. I am reading in the cinema magazine that the budget for making the show was miniscule, so it is extremely profitable for the producers.

After a few more adverts, *The Great St Trinian's Train Robbery* is about to start. Made three years earlier, it is a farcical tale of seemingly posh yet juvenile delinquents who cause mayhem at every opportunity. The main man is Flash Harry, the cockney 'spiv' who the girls have bottling and selling their homemade gin and putting bets on their rich father's horses.

As the minxy schoolgirls seek to express their femininity in a most overt fashion, it is all a bit too risqué for my liking. Harmless fun it may well be, but I am feeling a little inadequate here, if not a little overdressed.

Again, I am unaware that Miss Millicent Fritton, their headmistress, played by Alastair Sim, is also a man in disguise – working on the assumption that perhaps not all the women on the big screen necessarily had to be beautiful!

What is it with me and masked men, I have to ask myself? Perhaps it is because I am something of a mysterious girl myself (enough of the singing, that song hasn't been released yet) hiding behind a mask of virtuosity, when in reality I would prefer to be a victim of desire. After all was it not Mae West, the famous buxom blonde who suggested 'virtue had its own rewards' yet 'had no sale at the box office'? I think she may have had a point.

Zorro, the masked hero whose job is to 'defend people from tyrannical officials and other villains in the local vicinity', is my imaginary 'plus one' when I am on duty. I am smitten. Whilst his black eye mask conceals his identity, his presence is always revealed by the distinctive Z mark he leaves on his victims, having slashed them three times with his rapier.

As I stand here intrigued by this do-gooder, albeit with unorthodox practices, I am pondering over what the authorities would make of him if he were to hitch a ride with me in my time machine and end up in the 21st Century. Would he and the modern day 'hoodies' form some kind of allegiance, I wonder? After all they all operate in the same cunning and fox-like way when trying to escape capture. Might be best if he knocks the branding thing on the head methinks, if he doesn't want to add GBH to his list of charges.

On a different note, *The Man in the Iron Mask* – although not actually a cinema feature it is the one I sit and watch with my dad every Sunday night – is confusing the hell out of me. The trouble is, King Louis XIII has two sons and I am never sure if I am pining for good guy Philippe or his bad brother Louis, as they keep swapping over the masks, and it is awfully hard to keep track.

It would not be Saturday morning pictures without the rolling episodes of *Tarzan*. Give me Clark Gable, Rock Hudson or Tyrone Power over Johnny Weissmuller in the looks department any day, but the ape man needs credit where credit is due. It was the time when Tarzan first met Jane that had me believe in love at first sight and happily ever after, and quite possibly why I look for romance in every film I watch.

All showings over, it is now time to offload the strawberry Mivvi ice creams, ice-cream tubs and orange juice cartons and release the tray from around my neck, having been totally, if only momentarily, immersed in the magic of the cinema. 'Piff, Paff, Poof!' As I twitch my nose I am gone in a puff of smoke, landing right back behind my laptop in 2011.

In the world of entertainment, 1969 was the era in which Elvis completed his military service in Germany; when Eddie Cochrane died in a car crash; when comedian/singer George Formby died; when movie actor Ronald Reagan was elected Governor of California; when colour television was first broadcast in Britain; when actress Judy Garland died of a drug overdose in London (not in Kansas nor on the Yellow Brick Road); when novelist Enid Blyton died; and when the Beatles first released *Love Me Do*. It was also the time when the Bachelors' Summer Spectacular Show took place at the Victoria Palace Theatre, featuring comedians Dick ('ooh you are awful') Emery and Freddie 'Parrot Face' Davies alongside 16 high-kicking Tiller Girls.

It was also a time when I was sending in milk bottle tops to *Blue Peter* and sending off for biographies of my favourite movie stars to *Woman* magazine – I could get back three at a time, completely free provided I enclosed a stamped addressed envelope. I still possess the prized folder to this day.

Unfortunately nowadays the cinema has exhausted its appeal for me. Instead I prefer to watch films from the comfort of my laptop on DVD. With a little help from You Tube I have since learned how to set my PC Microsoft Oven so that I can eat and view at the same time. It involves little more than turning the dial towards mytv.din-din on the drop-down 'menu', setting the time to 8.5mins @75% heat and at the push of a button it will start/cook/get hot and hey presto, I am sorted. All I need is a Microsoft waiter to top up my Babycham glass and I will be in seventh heaven!

COMMERCIAL BREAK-UP

As I was growing up it would be fair to say that television was the main leisure pursuit in my life and for me the primary source of information. I was never much into 'educational' programmes – more 'escapism', as you may have already gathered, but I got to learn a lot about the film stars.

I can say in all honesty that sitting at home whilst others of my age were out getting up to all sorts of innocent antics was not my way of trying to blur out any sad, unpleasant or uncomfortable happenings in my life, as I had a wonderful childhood. Sitting on my grandad's knee whilst he rubbed his unshaven chin tenderly across my cheeks, *Watch with Mother* was a firm favourite of mine. My favourite was always Andy Pandy – a string-puppet baby clown who came to life when his owner was not around, and got up to innocent antics. His friends, Teddy and a rag doll called Looby Lou, would quickly scamper into a wicker picnic basket with him whenever his 'owner' came home. Fortunately he was not about to face a fate worse than death (if that is at all possible) and whilst he was free to leave that basket and any time, unlike poor Shmuel, I still think of him as the original boy in the striped pyjamas (Mark Herman, 2008).

Then there was Bill and Ben, the two 'flowerpot men' who also came to life getting up to all sorts of mischief while the gardener was away and then scurrying back into their respective pots at the sound of his footsteps.

And diddly dum, diddly dee, why is it that when talking to people of my generation about the 'olden days,' I seem to be the only one who can remember Sara's Hoppity? Surely someone else must remember the little girl who used to swing on the garden gate and who constantly got blamed for the naughty behaviour of her best friend – a one-legged marionette? Perhaps they were sending out subliminal messages like 'quick, quick, get back to the kitchen before Hubby gets home and catches you having fun!

I could never anticipate if his 'lordship' would come home early (he was the boss after all), so it would be hit or miss whether I could get to pop along to another universe now and then. Mid mornings I was thinking would be best as the roads would be quieter with the kids at school, but I would need to head back just before they came out in case I got caught in an orbital traffic jam. How could I explain that one away?

I feel like a 'Puppet on a String' some days as the sound of Sandie Shaw rings in my ears, but hey, I guess that is all part of normal matrimonial life. Having finished the hoovering, hung out the washing and prepared dinner it is time for me to have a little fun on Tracy Island.

Under my own identity I do not have, nor do I ever expect to have, my own chauffeur, but now, having assumed the role of Lady Penelope Creighton, I do. His name is Parker (his 'nibs' I call him – my 'pen' name for him, pun intended). Like me he is somewhat of a cockney yet, unlike me, he is the best safe-cracker and cat burglar in this imaginary town. Thank God I don't 'do' Facebook, I was thinking, else he might know I am away from home, hop into my time machine, go forward to 2011 and rob me blind!

Instead of the very basic five-door 'runaround' sitting on my drive, I am now swanning around in an iconic six-wheeled Rolls-Royce with a personalised number plate that reads FAB-1. In the words of Del Boy Trotter (who is yet to be heard of), this is 'triffic'!

I am experiencing a bit of Red Carpet TV here and loving it. The machine guns in the grill, the bullet-proof glass, the water skis for floating on water and the radar assisted steering are awesome, but the pink bodywork does not match my complexion very well – it makes me look a little anaemic!

The insurance here is high – I am not sure I can afford it, but it serves me right for going for a customised vehicle. What the heck! I have set up a direct debit to pay for it on an hour-by-hour basis as my fantasy won't last that long anyway.

At the Thunderbirds establishment I am having a field day playing at being a London agent for a secret organisation called International Rescue. It is much more fun than playing a drug dealer ordinarily, yet before I get arrested while my manuscript is still on the cutting room floor, 'she-who-administers-medication' might be a better way of phrasing it.

Parker is my loyal and indispensable assistant and complements my style of working very well. As Lady P, I have a kind but dinky little heart the size of an LED battery and I treat him well. He gets paid extremely well for his services, albeit with ink cartridges. Besides, he knows that if he doesn't come up to my expectations all I have to do is to cut his strings and there are so many other thunderbirding friends I can replace him with.

Captain Scarlett has been giving me the eye since I arrived, and whilst he is rather handsome he does not have any real structure to him and it has been said he has a wooden heart, so I am keen not to give off the wrong signals as I lower my gaze. In my *alter ego* world I need to be the one pulling all the strings in a relationship!

My time here is done. It has been pretty boring really, and I am concerned that the 'yellow peril' may slap a parking ticket on the machine before I can get back home. It is the 1960s and parking meters are new on the market.

With only minutes to spare before my passport ran out I was sitting back in the time machine, and as I pushed the lever on the dashboard I saw Tracy Island fade into the distance, landing me back to earth just in time to walk the dog. I knew I would see my thunderbirding pals again, and I was right. In 2001 I saw them on a DVLA TV commercial reminding people to pay their road taxes. Much like Shirley Valentine, who spoke to the microwave, I was talking to the 'box' saying 'hey, how you doing Parker? Remember me?' Needless to say I got no response, but as yet I have not been sectioned.

We all know that wedding rings are the world's smallest handcuffs. Perhaps that is why my *alter ego* needs to break free now and again.

Hubby arrived home half an hour later, having picked up the remote control before he had even taken his shoes off – that little gadget that enabled him to scan through umpteen channels at breathtaking speed only to complain there was nothing worth watching on the box. I had come to that conclusion a lot earlier, having browsed the TV mags.

Now out in the kitchen, knocking something up for lunch, I ask him what is on the television. 'Dust' I hear him mutter, sniggering at the same time, telling me it was on account of the fact that I was spending too much time on my computer and not enough time on the housework. Moi? Spending too much time on the computer? Poppycock! I was thinking to myself, 'any more comments about my housekeeping and you too might find yourself disposable, just like the Kleenex in those adverts showing in my time 'away'.'

OK, so perhaps I do need to take a few more commercial breaks from the laptop, but I really hate the flow of my creative juices to be interrupted and, perhaps I ought to spread the Mr Sheen a little wider in future. I will bear it in mind.

Now the poor old dog is running around in circles like a maniac and I am telling Hubby porky pies that I have been letting him in and out all morning so I don't get moaned at for neglecting another of my wifely duties, yet do feel awfully guilty on both accounts. OK Bert, says I. Let 'Mummy' go get your lead!

DOPEY AND MOUTHPIECE

So, widow Tracy's five adult sons, Scott, Virgil, Gordon, Alan and John, were dedicated to 'saving human lives', which was very commendable, but then so am I. I grew up reading the Famous Five and the Secret Seven, who concentrated more on 'saving the day' no matter what adventures they undertook and what unsavoury characters they got tangled up with. However, those were the kinds of books that sought to fuel my imagination for deductive reasoning.

As the eldest of five, and seven in later life, decidedly upper-class children we most definitely were not. Having turned the too-damp-to-sleep-in bedroom at the end of our second-floor council flat into a 'den' we used to spy, with our makeshift 'telescopes' made out of empty toilet rolls, not on smugglers but on the milkman, the potato man, the man from the Prudential or the rag 'n' bone man, depending on who had been seen walking across the 'no ball games allowed' courtyard and making their way along the balcony to our front door.

What fun we had in those days living on the less than affluent side of Highgate before tablets or mobile phones were invented. The neighbours were a little rough around the edges, but despite that they always referred to mum and dad as Mr or Mrs Kelly – respectful, to say the least. I could not have known at that point that I was going to get married, nor that those very same neighbours would have mucked in at sweeping up the autumn leaves and accumulative dust that had lingered around the courtyard for months as I proceeded to make my way in my wedding dress with enormous train in tow towards the waiting hired Mercedes that was to take me to the church from which I was to emerge as someone's wife.

Having tested Hubby no end of times on the difference between theft, robbery and burglary in preparation for his final police exam in previous months, I was already playing the part of his accomplice – that unintentional knowledge which remarkably I have been able to retain to this day. Don't expect that I should be able to quote the entire Police and Criminal Evidence Act though – the codes of practice that regulate police powers and protect public rights. Just let me 'PACE' myself a little when it comes to solving mysteries in my 'other' world.

So, as Wednesday arrives once more (my one mid-week day off from work), I need travel no further than my living room to be able to live out my fantasy at being a female sleuth.

The year is 2011 AD. I have squeezed myself into my 52-inch TV screen and am about to explore my options on the 'classic gold' channel. I need to decide which female detective character will suit my personality the best as I flick myself around the sets.

First stop is St. Mary Mead – a fictional village created by some author called Agatha Christie. Perhaps you have heard of her? Programmed to be focused and decisive at work, I am finding it extremely hard to come across as confused and 'fluffy' in my portrayal of Miss Marple. My skills at psychology are coming into their own however, as I set out to try to get into the minds of the villagers. I have been trained to study human nature and the lengths they might go to in order to get themselves out of bother – all this I must take into account if I am to solve the mystery of the murder at the vicarage which I have been called in to investigate. If I fail to solve it I shall be back in my garden pulling up weeds and will have to give back the tweed suit, so I need to give it my best shot, else Jessica Fletcher, my competitor, will start interfering in my case, and in good old TV fashion, murder will follow around what few friends I have, especially my overseas ones who live in Cabot's Cove.

Let's try a different studio.

I may not be an expert in plant biology, but I think I am wearing just as well as Felicity Kendall these days, so why not take over the role of Rosemary Boxer? I may not have led such a 'good life' as Felicity back in the 70s, but I have always been pretty self-sufficient and have rarely had to knock on the doors of any neighbours – albeit poor versions of the Leadbetters – for a cup of sugar. And besides, my natural curiosity and instinct for getting to the bottom of things rarely lets me down. I need some *thyme* to think!

Playing the part of Juliet Bravo is out of the running, as in a month of cockney slang I could never master a Lancashire accent and unless I can learn to pack a gun better than I can pack the shopping at Tesco, assuming the role of either Cagney or Lacy is also out of the window.

I need something juicy to get my teeth into. I have enlisted the services of a private eye called Rigby Richardson to help me prove that the reported death of my father in a mountain car crash was no accident. My assumed name is Juliet Forrest. This is the perfect chance for me to meet some of the Hallmark stars from the 1940s and 50s that I used to watch with mother, as I set out to learn of the friends or enemies that my father may have had in and around Carlotta. If only I had not forgotten my autograph book!

Just for the record, 'Carlotta' was 'the kind of town where they spelt trouble TRUBLE.' Could be that my father got killed simply for trying to correct the spelling! But there again I do not relish the thought of having to suck a bullet from Steve Martin's shoulder, at the risk of ruining my lipstick.

Besides, I know already that my father did not die

in a car crash. He died of bronchial pneumonia, and it was not in some mountain retreat but on a ward at University College Hospital in London in 1986.

To be honest, all I really want to do is to find out why *Dead Men Don't Wear Plaid* (1982). I thought this channel-hopping thing would be more exciting and I would find myself in a real sought-after role.

Just as I am about to give up I hear the telephone ring, so I jump right out of my TV set to answer it. The god-like voice at the other end tells me his name is Charlie and he runs a detective agency. It seems he has been contacted by a family member of one of my patients who has told him I work hard day in and day out for little reward and that this could be my chance to break away.

He tells me he is a millionaire who wishes to remain anonymous and that he has just opened his own private investigation agency and wants me to work for him. It is a mystery indeed. He wants me to work as a model, cocktail waitress or showgirl, as the situation dictates, having been updated on how bashful I am, and reassures me that any of the naughtier guises he would leave for Kate or Sabrina – his other 'Angels' – to fight over. How could I resist?

My smartness and strength at being a foil decoy and my skills at reverse psychology are beginning to come into their own. Seeking to lure and capture unsuspecting criminals as agent provocateur is something I am struggling with, however. The closest I have come to anything remotely alluring is the scent I spray lavishly on my person before a night out.

I begged Charlie to let me go back to my original day job caring for the elderly, who could see me in whatever light I wanted them to, depending on whether it was a full moon or not! This was my comfort zone, not the inside of a New York police department.

I was born way too late to play at being Mata Hari. I have neither the grace nor poise to become an artist's model or an exotic dancer, so that puts me out of the running as a double agent – a double cheeseburger with fries I could manage a lot easier. Besides, she was born in Paris and I in London, and I am not sure what the equivalent of 'femme fatale' is over here.

I did take up belly-dancing for a while, though god knows how I got talked into it. Hubby wasn't keen at first but was happy to let me walk out of the door knowing that I was well concealed and nothing much was revealed.

Just as Alice had wondered what her world would be like on the other side of the mirror's reflection, I was 'curiouser and curiouser' to find out what was so special about this kind of dance. As I stood in front of my looking glass for one day a week dressed beautifully and tastefully, I did not see boring old me – I saw a mystic princess. As one who is ordinarily quite staid, this was my one chance to break the rules by wearing unique costumes and dancing around to sublime music. A chance to interpret the rhythm of the drum solo, to accentuate hits, pops, locks and spins or to simply act with fluid grace.

With a beautifully-made rainbow chiffon resting across my shoulders and the sound of Tamally Maak echoing around the dance room, I had learned to master well the 'kiss cascade', the figure of eight and the front turbo. I had found my own Yellow Brick Road within a room above a bar. Not a pair of ruby slippers in sight as in those brief moments I imagined myself living in the old gypsy quarters of Sulukule, nestled within the walls of Istanbul.

Making my way across the road to where my car was parked, Hubby would joke that I could never get away with committing burglary as 'they' would hear me coming. He was referring to the gold coined hip-scarfs that I wore around my waist, yet I was thinking to myself, who in their right mind would go out and commit such a crime dressed like this? Sounds a bit like 'who lives in a house like this', doesn't it?

Getting ready in time each week was beginning to become a right 'Carry On', so my belly-wobbling days were numbered, but it was nice, I have to confess, to have been part of a 'fun' team, something I had not experienced since my days as a Brownie.

I have digressed somewhat, but the point I am trying to make is that I have not had a very successful day off today and whilst I have idealistically thought of my TV set as a window of opportunity allowing me to live out my fantasies as a television sleuth, I have failed miserably, and it is time to get back to the real world.

For someone who is still struggling to find out who really shot JR (there were nine likely suspects), who actually framed Roger Rabbit (so the cartoonist could wipe them out), who was responsible for the death of

Marilyn Monroe and what kind of smooth criminal paramedic administered that lethal dose of propofol to Michael 'Peter Pan', perhaps I should take a step back and carry on care-planning.

As for the Dopey and Mouthpiece title of this chapter – that's what Hubby called them. For those of you who are not old enough to recognise the reference, Dempsey and Makepeace were a police double act in the same way as Starsky and Hutch, or 'Smelly and Crutch' as his amusing 'take' on it. Ha ha! I am so not laughing.

CRIME PASSIONNEL

Frequently I could murder a glass of wine and more frequently my dearly beloved could murder a pint of ale. Isn't it criminal the price you have to pay for such social indulgences these days?

'I could murder you sometimes' I have told him many a time when he fails to bring down his dirty clothes until after I have put the washing machine on. Of course I did not mean it – no more than he meant he could 'strangle' me for using a metal spoon in a non-stick saucepan, having told me time and time again not to do so. Given our respective job roles, perhaps this was not the most appropriate use of words and taken literally could one day land us in sticky waters.

I have always wanted to go on a murder mystery weekend, but like everything else it is not always everyone's cup of tea (something else I could murder on a regular basis) so at the risk of having to go alone, it is something else that has had to be put on hold. That being the case, I have had little choice but to pretend I am a movie star who is hosting a VIP gala event for my multi-million-dollar up and coming movie release *Meurtre par jalousie*. In English that means murder by jealousy, but it somehow does not sound so criminal in French.

My inspiration for keeping the thread of my love and knowledge of the Hollywood movie stars running through my book is to play out a murder mystery 'game' – inspired by a party kit that I picked up in a car boot sale a few years ago. It's an old 1999 version of 'What the Butler Saw', but I need to recreate it in some way to fit my purpose.

So as I sit up in the bedroom creating away while he is sat downstairs watching *Band of Brothers* on DVD for the third time, it should be said from the outset that the crime of passion that I am about to create in no way bears any resemblance to real life. I have not yet found his lordship in bed with another, so I have not yet had to kill a romantic antelope. Oops, I mean interloper. You see, I cannot even get that right – so god knows how I could pull off the perfect murder.

But hey, I am not me for today. I am part of a movie that touches upon lust and romance in which I have cast Laurence Olivier as the Prince Regent and Marilyn Monroe as Elsie Maine. She is a showgirl. I am merely Larry's undying love interest. Does it sound familiar? I was barely a year old when that film came out and my retentive memory is not that good.

I have invited only the most prestigious of Hollywood stars to attend this special but as yet unannounced VIP premiere to promote additional media hype for my movie. As my guests arrive on the red carpet they are greeted with cocktails and appetisers. I have chucked in a few home-made vol-au-vents for good measure. Most of my celebrity guests already know each other. After mingling about and getting caught up in all the latest Hollywood gossip, I give them all a personalised gold laptop on which they can indulge in a fun 'What Movie Star Am I?' challenge on a fake social media application, on account that I do not own one. I ask them to write, direct, produce and act out their own little plays to entertain the rest of us, but not before they have indulged in the delectable star-worthy dinner that is about to be served – a time when my guests have already begun to collect information from and about the others to use in their scripts. The laughter is flowing as much as the champagne.

Then the candles flicker and the venue becomes a stage. Some of the guests continue to top up the posh cava and flirt with each other in true Hollywood fashion, whilst others are playing out their fantasies.

Suddenly the frivolities are interrupted when one of my maids announces that she has just found my leading lady dead in the conservatory. My very good friend the distinguished detective Philip Marlowe openly declares that he is about to come out of retirement for one night only, having assisted in that other case on the Orient Express. Underneath his wise-cracking and hard-drinking persona, he is a fantastic private eye, known for his quiet contemplation and philosophical manner. Although he knows he has already had one too many brandies he is trying to remain professional. He needs to consider all possibilities and keep an open mind.

Tongues are wagging in some quarters whilst the sound of laughter continues in others. In true Hollywood fashion no one really blinks an eyelid at my maid's revelation, more intent on posing for the paparazzi whilst competing for a front-page spread. One lady is going absolutely Gaga, as she cannot get a look in. I am not surprised – she is wearing a dress made of raw meat, and it stinks!

As Philip mingles with my guests his ploy is to loosen their tongues with liquor (that's alcohol to us Brits) with a view to being able to extract any information from them that might lead him to the culprit. Murder and motive are reportedly two very good friends of his.

Elsie (aka Miss Monroe's) photographer David Canover had made no secret that he was jealous of all the attention she had got from the armed forces, having participated in a recent photo shoot in order to 'help the war effort.' She had become the troops' 'eye candy', but when it came to Elsie giving him attention he felt it was being rationed.

Joe DiMaggio. Now here is a man who worships the

ground 'Elsie' walks on, but even though he turned up at the party accompanied by a stunning brunette, he had never quite got over it when she broke off their engagement.

'Elsie' has been teasing Joseph Cotton the entire evening, as she did before when they spent a few days at Niagara Falls. It had become public knowledge that he had been humiliated by her turning her attentions to a much younger man who knew her only as Rose and not Mrs Something.

Joseph was also feeling threatened at her continuous flirting, yet again, and had never quite got over everyone calling him a pushover. He had slipped out, relatively unnoticed, during the dessert.

Right in the middle of all this JFK and Jackie have arrived. I could cut the atmosphere with a knife. His affair with Marilyn, I mean Elsie, I mean Rose (by any other name) was a closely-guarded secret. Or so he thought. Could it be that his wife knew more than she had been letting on and was dead set on revenge (pun intended)?

This is the same lady who had left JFK standing outside her dressing room time and time again, often for up to an hour, while she put the finishing touches to her make-up. He was the President of the United States after all – he did not like her toying with him by keeping him waiting. But he knew she knew that he would wait as long as it took for her to come out, because he was absolutely besotted with her.

His reputation as her lapdog was something he was not able to play down. He had been on tenterhooks all night, yet he had not wanted to miss the premiere. Could it be that he just did not want to miss the finale?

When questioned by Philip about his relationship with 'Elsie', Arthur Miller was quite open in his response. 'Her sleeping pills and alcohol consumption' he said, 'have made her mortally injured in some way'. Yet he confessed that he loved her in spite of it; perhaps not the best choice of words, given the circumstances.

Anyone who is anybody has attended this gala, and most of them have encountered Marilyn at some stage in their careers. She was indeed a hard act to follow.

Philip has been my friend and confidant for many years, and if he does not know me by now then no one does. Hubby always says that the eyes are like windows to the mind and I am fearful that Philip can see right through me now.

Just as the clock is about to strike twelve he summons me to the games room, where Laurence Olivier is waiting. Laurence had been a priest before he opted to become an actor and it was here that he now hears my confession; that I was jealous of Elsie, the showgirl who lived the life of a princess, while I have had to live like a pauper. After all, I am just a nurse in real life; overworked and underpaid whilst she was overpaid, oversexed and bloody over here at the launching of MY new movie, not hers.

She did things to men that I could never hope to do. Even though she treated JFK abominably, he still told the press that 'when she walked into a room it was like the parting of the Red Sea'. She commanded the attention of men the world over and I was convinced she was after a mention in the Guinness Book of Records. She even had waiters drooling over her, wanting to stand near her, smell her fragrance and breathe the same air as she did. Well they would get that close, it was not hard.

I tell the retired priest and my detective friend that it just wasn't fair. This woman, dependent on prescription drugs and alcohol to comfort her emotional instability, was held in such high esteem as a result of her seductive ways and I was jealous, jealous, jealous!

Oops, I should say, *jalouse, jalouse, jalouse*; almost forgot my own plot!

Now I may not have personified Hollywood glamour in the way she did, nor have an unparalleled glow and energy, but hey, we brunettes need cuddling too you know.

Why should every gentleman at my bash prefer to latch onto this blonde? I too am a lonely girl with dreams, but unlike her I did not wake up every morning to find that my dreams had come true. Why wouldn't any of them listen to my Cinderella story?

Philip allowed me to make a quiet exit on my way to the Black Maria, where Elsie's body already lay (well, it saved having to order one of those long black 'cabs'). I cried a million love songs, but hey, it had been MY party and I could cry if I wanted to. First Ebenezer had stolen my thunder and now she was doing the same!

In case you are wondering, it wasn't video that

killed this Hollywood star; it was a box of Thornton's chocolates that were left over from Christmas. I knew 'Elsie' had a weakness for luxury treats, so having injected *Arsenic* into each and every one of them, using a hypodermic needle attached to a syringe that I had bought at Boots a few days earlier, I then proceeded to wrap the box in some *Old Lace*, knowing she could not resist the temptation to unveil it. I had made a point of telling her, and only her, where I had kept my secret stash. There were only three of the soft centres missing, but this was enough to finish her off, so this was a crime of passion with a twist. Instead of stealing my husband she had stolen the limelight and then my chocolates, so as far as I was concerned I considered it to be justifiable homicide.

I must ask Hubby what the penalty for malice aforethought is when he next comes upstairs to use the loo.

MAD DATE 5

TYPECAST

We're only a few pages into the book and you must be thinking what is going on in the mind of this crazy-ass writer. It will all make sense eventually, trust me.

Perhaps a little background information is needed first.

I had already decided by the time I was 13 that I was going to write a book, having watched at that age *The Diary of Anne Frank* on the television, the original 1959 version starring Millie Perkins. For any of you who have not heard of it, it told the true story of a teenage Jewish girl who had to hide with her family behind a bookshelf to escape capture by the Nazis during WWII.

Though I have spent the past 20 years also sleeping in the attic – the loft conversion, to be precise – it is not my intention to keep my work lying up there for the next god knows how many years before my family discover it, nor is it my intention that my book should be translated into seventy different languages. English will do nicely thank you.

I was a little older than 13 when I started to buy autograph books to send away to the film stars to sign, and unfortunately I know not what became of them. But I had started to keep a diary ever since my first school trip away to St Mary's Bay in 1969, and the cockle-shells that I collected on my first ever treasure hunt remain intact under the very, very yellow pieces of sticky tape, as do the postcards I sent home to Mum and Dad with five penny stamps on them. I had gone to great lengths to explain where my dormitory and the corner shop were in relation to the pictures on the postcards and signalled which parts of the camp were 'out of bounds.' Like they should have been any the wiser!

Bless! Reading it today, it is basically a blow-by-blow account of what time we got up and went to bed and what we had to eat, with drawn pictures in my diary of our dormitory star rating. But I guess all good novelists have to start somewhere.

As I moved into secondary school I knew there was only one way I could ever hope to get into the world of journalism (that was my goal), and that would be to learn to touch-type and get a certificate to show my potential. So when it came to choosing my options at the age of 16, I was delighted that typing was on the agenda. I can vividly recall the first-ever typewriter I learned on. It was an Olivetti. We had many in the classroom, well I say many, but in fact there were only about a dozen of us girls who wanted to learn the art and not all of them had the same typeface. The typewriters I mean, not the girls, but there again we did come in different shapes and shades. The typefaces were referred to as 'Pica' and 'Elite', with the basic difference being that the 'Pica' typed 10 characters per inch across whilst the 'Elite' produced 12 – but I am not about to give a blow-by-blow account of the workings of these machines.

How I used to love the sound of the old manual typewriter – the indispensable tool that was used by all professionals back then and I should like to think is still in use in some places today. It took an awful lot of effort to push down on the keys, although as a young lady I knew no different, yet my lack of dexterity these days would undoubtedly have me jamming more keys than I did 40 years ago. So whilst this literary hamster might still be able to run around an old keyboard, I might now be 'wheely wheely' slow by comparison. What I used to love most of all was hearing the bell that sounded when you got to the end of the line and using the carriage return lever to move the paper up to continue from where you had left off.

When, one Christmas, my parents had bought me my first-ever portable electric typewriter with carrying case (lift-off lid) I was ecstatic. However, the keyboard was a lot flatter than I had been used to and I thought I would never get the hang of it, much in the same way as I thought I would never get used to my first laptop, which I did not get to figure out until the year 2000.

I have heard it said many a time that a book is a lens through which a person can view themselves. Mum and I share the same blood group and the same DNA, so I guess we have always been on the 'same page'; that I have in some way inherited her genes of imagination, but with one big difference. Mum has always had this flair for writing wonderful poetry and would always create a verse to go inside Dad's birthday cards, as far back as I can remember. Poetry is not my field of expertise, I have to say.

At the age of five, Mum found herself standing on Paddington Station with a Mickey Mouse gas mask around her neck and a label as if she were a parcel, not knowing why and too young to appreciate that Britain was at war with Germany. Sending her away to live with strangers to avoid the possibility that her home might get bombed was the most heart-wrenching decision my nan and granddad had to make, and they were not even allowed to know the destination of their eldest child due to government secrecy.

She was one of the fortunate children to have been placed with a loving family, which is my only comfort. A little Cockney, born in 1934 in the London Borough of Tower Hamlets, within earshot of the sound of Bow Bells, she had lovingly been known in the village of St Wenn as 'Mrs Biddick's little maid', after the lady who had taken her in. As a defensive adult daughter I used to be upset by that title, having wrongly imagined for so long that this woman had Mum working like a servant in exchange for her keep. As time wore on, however, and she told me tales about her growing up on a farm, of helping out with the harvest, of chasing headless chickens around the farmyard and drinking hot frothy milk straight from her very own cow Daisy, I felt so much better.

The memories of her childhood sweetheart John during those 'wonder years' never faded, but he went on to marry one of the young ladies in the village, who still remained there long after Mum returned to London after the war. I was very privileged to have met the man who had stolen her heart 70 years ago when my sister Antonia had arranged a reunion for Mum at the very same house where she had stayed all those years ago and she had invited me along to share in the moment.

Mum had been educated very well in the village whilst living at a place called Treliver, and on her return to London after the war she went on to take the Eleven Plus exam and got a place at Hornsey High School. It was an all-girls' grammar school back then and she exceeded in all her lessons, especially English, typing and shorthand. In 1997 she wrote a poem about her time as an evacuee, a copy of which now lies in a historical museum, and I share it here. So you see, I have my mother to thank for my perseverance in all I try to achieve.

EVACUATED

How clearly I remember
That day so long ago
When as a child I went away
From those who loved me so
A steam train took us all away
From London's danger zone
To live with strangers far afield
To a second home
I still recall so clearly
The country village hall
Full of children waiting, hoping
For that special call
The call that you are wanted
To join a family there
Someone who would love you
And take you in their care.

I was very lucky
For six long years I stayed
Upon a Cornish farm
Where I became a Cornish maid!
I played among the primroses
And plucked the daffodils
And harvest time was wonderful
On golden, rolling hills
I soon forgot the sounds of war
And life for me was sweet
I walked to school through country lanes
Enjoyed the summer's heat.

And when the war was over
And I knew that I must go
Back to a London I hardly knew
To those who loved me so
I cried for those I had to leave
The ones I loved so dear
But thoughts of them, of bygone days
Will always keep them near.

Doreen Grace Kelly, 1997

Despite having been an evacuee for all those years, she was determined that this would not stop her from making the most of her education, and when she went on to get a top job working as a secretary at Hulton Press from 1953 onwards, she was in seventh heaven. It is no wonder that she was so happy and willing to indulge me in keeping scrapbooks of the old movie stars, especially as she had a little secret that I was not to learn until I had got a little older. Working on the *Picture Post* magazine, Mum had been in the privileged position of being able to get all the latest film illustrations and had held on to her vol. 4, No. 9 fifteen-pence edition with Farley Granger on the front. Not only that, she went on to become penfriends with the man who was to be one of MGM's finest recruits. He went on to secure a seven-year film contract with Samuel Goldwyn following his portrayal of a 'romantic juvenile' opposite actress Jane Withers in *North Star*, although I have to confess I have not yet seen it. It was a special kind of 'penpalship' (now there's a new word for the Oxford Dictionary). Mum never got to meet the man. His letters are quite personal, but it was so unlikely that he would turn up unannounced on her doorstep that even after she married Dad he never expected her to be parted from them. In fact Dad would have been the first one to have put the kettle on if it had happened – after he had picked Mum up from the floor.

Having raised seven children over the years it was evident that thoughts of her 'heart-throb' were never far away, as we all grew up with Farley's rusks!

Those letters are her prized possessions, and should it turn out that they are worth anything in times to come, perhaps she will give me enough to allow me to get my book covered in gold lame, if it ever takes off! The letters and photos of Farley are reproduced on the centre pages.

In the meantime, how does all this talk of typing fit in with my fantastical world of entertainment, I hear you ask? After all, this is what you came here for isn't it?

Well, my mission (should I choose to accept it) is to dig into my crazy mind and think about how the film industry had inspired me to go on and become a secretary in my own right. Before I became a wife and mother I worked as a PA for a company called Marley Vehicle Leasing, but rest assured my boss most certainly did not drag a heavy chain around the office to denote any greed or selfishness on his part, nor could the other senior manager have been accused of being a Scrooge, as he often brought in rum babas from the little pastry shop not a million miles away. Mind you, there was this one guy who used to remind me of Uriah Heep on account of his lanky frame and equally greasy and lanky hair.

What the Dickens has this got to do with anything I can hear you say? Nothing really, except I have been thinking how I can link the typing skills I was able to utilise back then with my imaginary world of a TV film star. Let me see...

I could get Kate Winslet to hand over her secretarial and administrative role in the film *Enigma* to me in exchange for a piece of the deck from the *Titanic* upon which she had danced with Jack. It will be ace to try my hand at stealing the super-sized typewriter that the Nazis were using during the war in order to be able to send coded messages to each other. I could have great fun trying to unscramble those messages, just to be able to prove to the enemy that their encryptions are not impenetrable to my fellow Brits. Of course, I may need to spend a few hours researching how to use the notched wheels (there are three but could be as many as five, I believe) and how to rotate them so that they display different letters of the alphabet, but hey, I can operate a QWERTY keyboard of 26 letters and the rest, so it should be a doddle. I might even be able to apply for the role as a stand-in for Miss Moneypenny at the point where she has to relinquish her secretarial duties and return to the Women's Royal Naval Service.

Working for the head of the British Secret Society, I would do my mysterious boss 'M' proud, and whilst I would be utterly dedicated to my work and not indulge in too much social activity that might compromise confidentiality, I wouldn't be able to promise that a little harmless flirtation with 007 (just so long as it was Sean Connery) wouldn't be on the cards, but all I would be after is the key to his Martini cabinet!

Failing that, I could always apply online to become a virtual assistant. Home would be my office, I could start and finish when I wanted and take my tea breaks at whim.

Oh well, maybe not. I shall have to stick to completing hand-written care plans at work, where I don't have to have crane-like legs or wear killer heels, and besides, my other half needs me around to help him type up his contingency plans in a way that only I know how, else he will take all day using his two index fingers.

I have always wondered whether, in my spare time, I could possibly keep up with Jerry Lewis and his air-typing antics whilst minding the store. It is pretty cool and I can do 78 words a minute, just for the record!

Hang on. I have just turned my computer on and those three magic words are flashing up: 'You've Got Mail.' Is it from Tom? No, wait! It is from the GPO telling me I have a letter waiting for me to collect from the sorting office, as it was too large to go through my letterbox. There goes another romantic dream!

And yes, I do go into my own little world at times, but it is fine because everyone knows me there.

MAD DATE 6

LET ME CALL YOU SWEETHEART

There may be times when I feel like packing up my troubles in an old kit bag and forcing a smile, smile, smile; but then as I sit here writing my memoirs, wading through memories past and present, I am thinking that life is not so bad after all.

I had a very brief interlude with military life within the Territorial Army, during which a young man who had set his sights on me from day one proposed to me three months later, telling me he knew at our very first meeting that I was the girl he was going to marry. I did not mind in the least when he insisted I hand in my uniform, fearful that someone might 'steal his girl'.

'Pass us another beer, girl' says that very same man now, looking at me from across the living room as we head towards our ruby wedding anniversary, the jade necklace and earrings which he could not wait to give me lying on the dining table as we speak.

I could sit here and say that my inspiration for signing up came from having spent much of my time watching the old British war drams with my parents as a young lady, but this really wasn't the case. I would rank my old time favourites as *Odette, Carve Her Name With Pride, Millions Like Us* and *Mrs Miniver* high upon the list of 'culprits', although if truth be known, joining the ranks of the 39th City of London (Royal Signals) Corp in 1975, which got me out of the house for a couple of hours a couple of nights a week (and for which I got paid) was to fill in the time when I was not sitting replying to penfriends who I had gathered from all over the world through a weekly magazine.

I cannot physically leave the house to hop into the time machine and go back to the 1940s, as I know I shall not get back in time before he asks me to pass him the Chinese takeaway menu. Don't get me wrong – he is not a lazy chap and readers might consider that I am no more than a 'fetcher and carrier', but I am an old-fashioned girl and just act instinctively, feeling very much needed, so do not worry for me.

Had we been blessed with a twelve-bedded mansion with several storeys, I could likely disappear into one of them right now and he would be none the wiser if I didn't put in an appearance for a while and would be very lenient towards my poor old legs, as they would take a while longer to hobble down the long and winding staircase. Since this is not the case, I will be very conspicuous by my absence.

Don't get me wrong. One thing I am not is materialistic. I am happy with my little house in a cul-de-sac somewhere in the West Country. I was not born with a silver spoon in my mouth. No silver Mercedes (but for that hired one on my wedding day) ever adorned the roadside of that little council estate where I spent the best part of my premarital life growing up, just my old Mini 850 cc, TUC 868F – one of the few number plates I can still remember 46 years on. I still have the old tax disc tucked away somewhere.

To those who have never lived in London it can be a city that may seem alien, confusing and unfriendly, but it was never like that back in 'my day'. It has changed a lot, granted, but no matter how much I have moved around the country with my husband when following his career, in my mind it will always be 'home' to me.

I once heard seventeenth-century Chelsea described as 'a village of palaces', a place where investment bankers and film stars 'hung out.' It remains today a similar place of influence and affluence. Whilst it was not compulsory that I should support Chelsea Football Club with three brothers and a tomboy sister among our brood, it was high on my agenda. Besides, supporting CFC was a mark of being a true Londoner, and they were the most influential team around. Dad would frequently take the boys to the matches whilst

I would contemplate running up skirts by hand for my sisters to wear, with the help of a Simplicity pattern.

To this day I have still not been to that part of London – but I'd bet my bottom dollar that even back in the 60s and 70s sitting on a bench by the roadside eating fish and chips out of a newspaper would have been frowned upon, and I dare say the same would apply today.

Peter was the 'in' name in the 70s and whilst the boys were cheering on the likes of Bonetti, Osgood and Lorimer back then, I was measuring the Petersham ribbon to sew into the top of an A-line skirt. Charlie Cooke was the one I swooned over, and Mum would have to buy endless packets of PG Tips in the hope that he would be among the free cards that came with them.

So I may not be an actual Chelsea Pensioner, but I am heading in that direction. My brothers continue to support the team to this day, and whenever the team are on the 'box' I cannot resist having a quick peep at the score, even though I do not feel the same sense of romance towards any of the players since my Charlie hung his boots up.

It was however, still the team that aspired me to create my own logo for a website that never quite got off the ground at a time when I was looking for a Chelsea hip-scarf on eBay so I could wow my belly-dancing instructor, but I always say 'never say never'.

The closest I ever came to royalty per se was standing at Kings Cross station every day waiting for the outward bound train to Farringdon, where I worked in an office adjacent to St. Paul's Cathedral and a stone's throw (pun intended) from Hatton Garden jewellers, where I brought an eternity ring for the man who was to be my future husband.

The only palace I frequented as a child, and then a young woman, was the one which is famous for its iconic radio tower, still today referred to as 'the people's palace', but to me it will always be 'Ally Pally', the place where Dad would take me to watch the horse racing and we would sit and eat monkey nuts in the stands.

Well, I most certainly will not be inconspicuous in my writing in a bid to keep the thread going now, will I?

Where was I? Oh yes, I was about to say that since I cannot physically travel back in time to meet up with my old 'black and white' film buddies, so I shall seek them out on the Paragraph Avenue. But first I shall pour some Cherry B into a glass – the aroma that evokes memories of the first drink Hubby bought me at the Lynx club at TA on our first-ever meeting. See how cleverly I am making the link?

Right, so there his lordship sits, poised this Sunday afternoon to watch *Zulu* for the umpteenth time, which means I have around three hours in which to get to Bobbington and back. I have assumed the role of the 'Forces Sweetheart'. I have put Vera Lynn into retirement and forced Katherine Jenkins back into the womb. It will soon be raining men now that the Prime Minister has announced that 'Britain is at war with

Germany'. All the serving soldiers, sailors and airmen have automatically become mine – a captive audience, so to speak.

Being a true Brit, it only seems right and fitting that the venue for my concert should be RAF Halfpenny Field in Halfpenny Green. The locals have got used to planes being shot down in the locality. It has become normal, and in living each day as if it was their last (hey, that record has not been made yet either), when the inevitable does happen, they take it in their stride, maintaining a stiff upper lip and call it a 'jolly bad show, old chap'. I am feeling apprehensive.

I could just afford to board the Chattanooga Choo-Choo. I have the fare and a trifle to spare (the one left over from yesterday's meal). I left my local railway station about a quarter to four, read a magazine and now I am in Exmoor; I am taking dinner in the diner, nothing feels finer, than having my ham and eggs in Little China (which just for the record, is a Peking and Szechuan restaurant in Littlewick Green, Berkshire), where we have made a quick stop.

Having finally arrived, on peering through the stage curtains I am eager to see who has accepted the invitation to my bash. As those bluebirds fly over the white cliffs of Dover, there in the front row is David McCallum (the man from U.N.C.L.E has given him the day off), Robert Wagner (I am looking forward to having a 'Hart to Hart' with him after the show) and Christopher Neame, who has recently resigned from filming *The Secret Army*. Between them they had managed to impersonate the German guards, feign insanity, make skeleton keys, forge German passports and draft maps using lemon jelly just so they could be with me today. How honoured am I that they have gone to all this effort to escape the impregnable fortress that is Colditz Castle, just to keep me happy.

David Tomlinson turned up a short while later. The guys told me he was their main man. He had this great knack at being able to hide sand in bedknobs and broomsticks and then disperse it into allotment fields when working outside the jail.

Sitting next to them are Cary Grant and Tony Curtis, accompanied by a handful of Philippine refugees and several gorgeous nurses. Guess he was looking forward to Operating on their Petticoats after the show.

But hey, who was I to take the moral high ground, having being very selective with my invitations, which were largely male orientated! Cary, however, had brought his schoolteacher mistress Leslie Caron along for the ride and I promised to help her find the secret stash of booze that this Father Goose had locked away on his boat by plying him with alcohol after the show in order to get a confession out of him. If he could be so easily enticed by the Navy with liquor in exchange for secretly monitoring and reporting back Japanese activity from his dilapidated vessel, then this should be a doddle.

I might as well have been reaching for the sky when I put out my invitation to Douglas Bader, who was the most courageous and determined person I knew, and seeing him walking down the aisle on his two artificial legs right now is awesome.

Sick of being around fools and carthorses and having said 'Goodnight Sweetheart' to both his 20th and 21st century wives, Gary Sparrow (aka Rodders) arrives. Cushty! He takes a seat in the back row, presumably because if he feels a sudden urge to go and walk through any brick walls, he will not disturb the others.

'It ain't 'half hot in ere Mum,' I hear Battery Sergeant Major Williams shout in his gruff Welsh voice as he marches towards the stage, with a swagger stick under his arm. He is followed by his long-suffering punka wallah Rumzan, who is attempting to keep him cool with a high-powered battery fan purchased on the Burmese equivalent of eBay. 'Back home' this would have been a gigantic palm leaf on a piece of string but hey, when in Rome and all that!

Rumzan's rendition of *Land of Hope and Glory* has my guests roaring with laughter, although Sarge tells him more than once to 'shut up' in a tone which makes poor old Muhammed, the Char Wallah, shake in his boots as he pours him endless cups of tea from the portable (cordless) kettle/teapot that had been bought from the duty-free shop at the airport before the flight over.

Pardon the comparison, but we have not had an 'Indian' summer for a long time and I am not about to turn the central heating off in the marquee for anyone.

La-Di-Da Graham and Lofty can't make it, I am told, as they are needed to hold the fort back in the jungle. They are not *that* big celebrities, so there is no chance of them getting out of there anytime soon. No worries. I do not have an exhaustive supply of seats, and besides they are reserved for the guys of 617 and 633 Squadron, but as it happens they cannot now come as they are needed to practise bouncing bombs back home – Operation Chastise I think it is called – as opposed to bouncing up and down in their seats to my medleys.

Having managed to Save Private Ryan and tell his little shopgirl that she must mind the bookshop herself for a little while longer after he 'got an email' from her on his iPhone, Captain Miller (I mean, Tom Hanks) waltzes in. This is indeed 'Big' of him I am thinking, as the sound of Chopsticks and visions of him hopping from one foot to another come to mind and if I could have got a walking piano into the tent then I would have. Besides, how old did he think he was – 12?

Elvis turned up, but he looked a little shook up to find my audience was predominantly male. He looked hellishly sad. It was evident then that he had a touch of the GI Blues. I could soon cheer him up.

Wow, Ben Affleck, the cherry on top of all my cakes, has just walked in, looking pretty hot considering he has just got back from a mission in Pearl Harbour. I had reports that he would not be able to make it, but it turns out some German had set his cockpit on fire (painful) and that his attempts to bail out had gone wrong when the canopy got jammed and his plane went down over the English Channel. It had been assumed he was dead to his Memphis belles back home, but that is what he wanted them to believe as a deliberate ploy to enable him to stay for one night longer and come to my concert hall. So smitten was I – he was bringing out the minx in me.

I had my usherette (who I had met during my days working in the cinema and whom I had kept in contact with all these years) pass him a secret message from me. It said he had better not sit under no English apple tree with anyone else but me and that if he played his cards right his plane would not be the only thing that would be on fire. There would be no need for J-Lo to find out, right? Nor Hubby for that matter – but since he is glancing at me from across the living room as I speak, he would never believe what might have happened in any case.

'The Yanks are coming, the Yanks are coming!' echoes around the tarpaulin as Richard Gere and William Devane swagger in like they own the place.

Now this is all well and good, but I am not a Yank. I am a limey and I need to call my fellow Brits to 'prayer' in the only way I can think how. So as my pianist warms up my audience with a rendition of *This is the Army Mr Jones*, Captain Mainwaring appears with his platoon, equipped with wooden guns and wearing armbands that denote they are Local Defence Volunteers. 'Jonesy' – a butcher at any other time – lags one step behind his boss as always.

Private Pike might well need his scarf, as it will get chilly in the big tent later on. I am grateful that Private Godfrey's sisters Dolly and Cissy have stamped his pass to leave Cherry Tree Cottages for one night. I am keeping a watchful eye on Private Walker – I don't want him flogging any dodgy gear to my friends when I am not looking, and I certainly hope that 'Frazer' has not come as a bad omen and that my efforts to bring joy to the troops as part of the war effort will not turn out to be 'doooomed'.

Like an idiot, I had the guys (and the few gals) hang their gas masks up in the cloakroom but I am thinking how so alike they all look, as do their cloakroom tickets, so I am preparing myself for the mayhem on collection. Still, we'll cross that Bridge over the River Kwai when we get to it, eh?

As everyone eagerly awaits the start of the show, I am still awaiting the arrival of Glenn Miller, who is going to be my musical partner for the evening – 'morale boosters', we like to call ourselves. He promised me he would fly to Paris on his way from the US to get some duty-free drinks to bring along for this evening, but it seems Frazer's influence has already kicked in as I read the content of a telegram that my old 'Ushy' friend has just passed me.

Sitting here greeting my guests one by one, I had not ventured outside for some time, so I could not have known what the weather was up to. It seems that no sooner had Glenn left RAF Twinwood Farm in Bedfordshire (drinks loaded and all) the weather had become 'real bad' – foggy as hell – and that his plane just disappeared over the English Channel. I am no longer 'In the Mood' for entertaining, but everyone had come such a long way and gone to a lot of effort, so the show needs to go on. To make matters worse my piano player has slipped out to the loo but has not returned. I will get a search party together to flush him out later. Maybe he has disappeared down the pan!

But all is not necessarily lost. I am straight on the mobile and the operator (none of this 118 118 lark) has connected me straight to Rick's Café in Casablanca (sod the roaming charges, I am thinking) and before I can say 'boo' to a Father Goose a flying camel has just landed outside the marquee with both Rick and his good friend Sam on board. Sam is a whizz on the piano and as a nightingale sings in Berkeley Square, we are churning out the old numbers and making the very best of a bad situation.

We are hanging out the washing on the Siegfried line, vowing there will always be an England, checking that lemon jelly 'sourced' map to see if it really is a long way to Tipperary, in agreement that no fag breaks will be taken underneath the arches at the risk of fire from all those cigarette butts, and shouting out into the dead of night, 'run rabbit, run rabbit, run, run, run before you all end up in a stew.'

As the minute's silence as a tribute to Glenn has ended, a Pilot Officer – his name is Peter Penrose, I believe – stands up and asks if he can recite a poem in memory of his friend Johnny. He asks that we do not despair for his colleague who has now found his 'Way to the Stars' having been unable to survive the terrible odds that all the boys home and abroad are still facing as bomber pilots as this wretched war continues.

As the flash of exploding shells can be seen in the sky, it is time for everyone to leave and find a safe place of shelter. With so many guys from all the different military backgrounds sitting under one roof I am concerned there might be conflict. Unknown to everyone, my dearest friend Jack Warner had been sitting right at the back of the marquee, next to 'Rodders', but fortunately for him he was able to enjoy his night off. However, he needed to be back at Dock Green the next day, so he needed to head off pronto. 'Evening all' he said, bidding them all a fond farewell.

I may have not been blessed with flaming red hair nor have a 38-inch bust or million-dollar legs, but hey, I think I did a good job, and many of the guys have asked if I will be their 'pin-up' girl after they get home.

'Cheering the boys who are winning the war' – this is what this pin-up girl will be for, not for any hanky-panky I can assure you and I hope they will watch where they put those drawing pins (or thumb tacks, as the Yanks call them).

Don't laugh at me as I take the final sip of my Cherry B. In fact you should be saluting me as it was a small bottle after all and I have managed to make it last through an entire war. You see I also know every word in that film, and he is not taunting me but teasing me by saying he doesn't want a Chinese takeaway now he wants me to cook. Go back to Rourke's Drift, I am thinking to myself.

He was joking of course, you will be pleased to know, and as I sit here pondering over what to order I am thinking to myself, 'Shall I have the Singapore chow mein, yung chow special fried rice, salt and spicy chicken and sweet and sour king prawn balls (dry) or should I add some chips to that?'

I will add some chips to that – after all I have been living on rations for the past three hours or so since he had chosen to spend his time with a bunch of Zulus rather than me, and now I am famished. And I will have a glass of wine with that when it arrives as my throat is still dry from all that singing!

MAD DATE 7

REEL ESTATE

So we have established that I do not live in a mansion as I have always dreamed of doing, or likewise that little house with a white picket fence, although it is quite feasible I could rig one of those up outside in a matter of seconds.

Serendipity – 'The effect by which one accidentally stumbles upon something fortunate, especially while looking for something entirely different.' Was it a serendipitous find, I wonder, that took me to the Never Never Land website last week as I consider my options for turning the wooden doll's house that Hubby bought me last year into something unique? And had it been

Mum in the 1950s

Another early photo of Mum

Mum at Hulton Press

The picture Mum sent to
Farley Granger

Farley Granger on the front of Film Illustrated

Movie posters
featuring Farley

A Christmas card from Farley

To Mum from Farley

Farley Granger P.O. Box 1126 - Studio City, California

Farley Grangerettes International

Honorary Member
F. G. I.

Hello! This is Farley. How are you?
Thank you very much for wanting my
picture. Do you like this one?

Your name has been entered as an "Honorary
Member" of the "Farley Grangerettes International"
if you don't mind, that is.

This is not a "Fan Club". There are no rules.
There are no dues. There are no obligations.
It is merely "my personal" "roster" of the
names and addresses of you swell "Gals"
who are writing to me from all over the
world, and whose warm interest makes
a fellow like me feel mighty humble.

It is nice to know who and where friends
like you are, and I would like it very
much if you will tell me from time to
time, your likes and dislikes for my
work and the type of roles in which I
am being cast.

I must depend upon you — because, you
are the folks I am really working for,
you know.

Thanks again for everything — (and
thanks to the many of you, who are
sending me your picture.

Deliberately Yours,
Farley Granger.

A Farley Fan Club letter

Sept. 5. 1953

"gray to hear about your friend."

Hi, Doreen: Its, me again! and I hope this reaches you before you leave on your holiday. Have a wonderful time huh?

I am writing this for two reasons, First to thank you for your nice letter as usual, and the snap-shots. All were mighty nice — but you know something? I like the one at th beach the best, but, have one complaint you are entirely too far distant from the camera, and I hope you will not think me "forward" if I say you certainly have no reason to be so ultra-modest. I mean it as a compliment. So do better next time, but — and come "closer"?

P. O. BOX 1126
STUDIO CITY, CALIF.
Farley Granger

Letter to Mum

Secondly, can I suggest something as a personal friend, for you to advise me & O.K.? I know you will understand.

I get many letters from all over the world, from kids who enclose a foreign stamp, or more, for pictures etc. These stamps have no value in the U.S. and I am wondering if you would care to have an accumulation of British stamps I have. Perhaps you can use them, or, make some disposition of them, as they are of no use over here, though uncancelled. Only one thing, you must be true to me, and not use them to write other actors. Promise? Do you wish them?

And, get a little more "reckless" with that camera, huh? Bye. Doreen, Farley.

Doreen:— This is to remind you of your promise long, long, ago you was sending me a "larger" pin-up. And and if you are happy I have forgotten you are wrong— I really believed I was a "favored" one. Or, will I only get this one back? Come now — no more excuses.

Thanks for your nice letters in the past Doreen, and I hope you and yours have a swell Xmas.

Farley Granger,

Have you seen "Naked Street — Girl in the Red Velvet Swing" or Senso? I am wondering if they have been released in England. Always Farley.

Another letter from Farley

Dear Doreen:
Thanks for your nice letter — and keep happy, huh?
Farley.

Personal note on the back of a fan club leaflet

Original envelopes from Hollywood

Hubby - the new recruit

The newly-wed

The fisherman

The fisherman

even more of a find that 'London's Biggest Little Toyshop', which the site introduces, just happens to be based in the very place I was born?

The site had been there all this time, yet I never knew it before now. Is it pure coincidence at the sad loss I feel for Michael Jackson who died a couple of years ago, and who was a significant part of my growing up, that I should now find myself going through the gates of Windows Vista towards that land of Oz where, once inside, 'the human world outside ceases to exist'? I believe you, Michael. Never Never land is a real place after all, but it is in North London, not Hollywood as you had been led to believe.

As the proud owner of a four-roomed Georgian style dolls house, therefore, arranged on two floors, I am about to enter the world of miniature Reel Estate (yes, that is the correct spelling for the purpose of my exercise).

Not one to follow a traditional theme, I need to consider one that fuels my imagination for decoration. I could turn it into a 1940s pub (as in *Goodnight Sweetheart* – I had discreetly asked Gary about the décor when I met him at the bash in Halfpenny Field); a modern-day cocktail bar; a sweet shop; or even an Indian restaurant. The latter seems the best option, since I consider myself something of a connoisseur, having been in just about every curry house in my locality when trying to source the best phal that my money can buy.

At that point there is interference in my brain activity (you don't say) as the words 'Georgian', 'Georgia', 'Deep South', 'Civil War', and more importantly 'Tara, Tara, Tara' echo inside my head. Or was it 'Tora Tora Tora' (nope, wrong war).

So the answer was starring me in the face (anatomically in the same region). My condominium will become a film studio within which four different film sets can be created within one – made to my own 'spec' and with precision, using my all-time favourite films as inspiration.

My own little 'property' may not be located in a prestigious area of North London within a conservation area or with a mature landscaped setting accessed via a private driveway fitted with electronic gates, but at £180 all in (Hubby had left the price on the box) it is something of a 'snip' in comparison to its £375,000 counterpart in the real world.

My artistic vision will be met with wood, nails and paint. With a little attention to detail, practice and a few tricks of the trade (Dad was a painter and decorator after all, so I have good insight), my responsibility for completing it to his lordship's liking will go beyond simply building the sets but will seek to become a living, breathing and fully detailed 'world' to which I can escape from time to time. Of course it would mean sourcing out a miniature scaled time machine also, but hey let's not run before I can fly eh?

The best thing of all is that I shall not need any planning permission, even when wanting to lay the first slab when it comes to creating my very own Yellow Brick Road.

Recreating a cyclone might be tricky, but I am sure I will be able to source out a Scarecrow, a Tin Man, a cowardly-looking Lion, a miniature Dorothy and Toto and of course a Wicked Witch of the West on that marking site – just so long as they come in one-twelfth scale! However, in order to make my work look authentic I need to do some serious research first.

As luck would have it (although he did not see it that way), Hubby has been signed up to a firearms course, which is to take him away from home for three days. Perfect, I am thinking. Now I will be free to sit and write from my heart, write from my crazy soul and try to make the best of my talents both as a writer and a builder.

Hubby loves to hog cooking the Sunday roast, but not as much as he likes to hog the TV remote, as you have already gathered. However now it will be my chance to take over the control once he leaves.

That day had not come a moment too soon, and I was faced with the strangest of things after I had retrieved it from down the side of the chair upon which he had last sat. Instead of channels it has time dates (mad dates as I call them, since this fits in nicely with my state of mind) and it is all but commanding me to uncover the time machine that is parked up in the garden by the side gate under some old membrane left over from when the decking was put up and where it had become necessary to replace the grass with stones because Bert, our border collie, had churned it all up whilst looking to round up imaginary sheep. I know, crazy eh? There again I do have flamingos in my garden, but that's a story for later.

Having watched *Gettysburg and Glory* with me other 'arf several times, I had a rough idea of what the Yankee Civil War was all about, but like all Hollywood movies it was over-romanticized, which is why I focused on the good and not the gore when watching them. My all-time favourite film, *Gone with the Wind*, was set in the same American Civil War, and this was where my research was about to get interesting.

So this is the thing. In the days before Hubby had gone away, I had seen a press release in some glossy film magazine. Some guy called Victor Fleming was looking to direct a film that would be set in the deep American south during that very same era. Vic was looking for someone who could play the part of a manipulative woman who has a turbulent affair with a loveable rogue, yet the prime candidates for the role of Scarlett O'Hara, Lana Turner, Kathryn Hepburn and Joan Crawford, had failed miserably during the mock scenes when they were having to look after the casualties as the battle continued.

It was the producer who had the idea to go undercover and seek out talent in the most obscure places, and I had told my manager that there was something quite strange about the distinguished-looking gentleman who had come to look around our place on behalf of his elderly mother, who was in need of 24-hour nursing care. I had offered him a cup of tea when he arrived but then carried on with my drug round. He never came back and the phone number he had left did not exist – well, not in this century.

Having brushed the cobwebs off the time machine I do not use the column change this time but have taken along the remote control, which has miraculously transformed itself. Having clicked on the 19th century button, I have landed right in the middle of 1867. My looks have undergone a radical change, as I now find myself on the right side of 20 and living an idyllic life at a North Georgian cotton plantation called Tara. Hey, I recognise this name from somewhere.

I am now beautiful but remain unspoilt. Pouting comes easily to me (Hubby always teases me about that when he winds me up), and my middle of the road temper remains, as does my strong-willed personality, but a shameless flirt has now emerged. At the lavish ball I am throwing the smell of testosterone is making me feel sick, but I continue to tease all those who are gathered around me drooling like babies cutting their first teeth, as they wait patiently whilst I decide which ones I will allow to do the Argentine tango with me.

My charming ball gown from ASOS swirls gently in folds of exquisite red silk around my waist, diamonds and an elegant array of white lace that delicately caresses my neckline. Who can resist me? I have a different home now and a different way of life, so my old clothes can go to the local jumble sale that is to be held on the edge of the estate at the weekend, I believe.

None of my admirers have the looks of Ben Affleck nor the sex appeal of George Clooney, but Ashley –

well, it really does not matter that he looks like an older version of Ed Sheeran on account of his red hair. He is kind, caring yet quietly charming and does not know that I have been harbouring a secret love for him for years.

However, I overhear tittle-tattle that he is about to marry his cousin Melanie and I am overcome with grief. She is as demure and sweet-natured as am I in real life, but I am not me (someone throw me a Snicker bar), I am Scarlett. I am from aristocratic stock, unlike Mel, and I am green with envy. I know Ashley wants me, but he does not know it yet, so when this guy called Rhett turns up at the ball boasting the most terrible reputation with the ladies, I cannot help, in a bid to make Ashley jealous, but respond to his cheeky attractive gaze which is directed my way.

All everyone is talking about is the war and it is spoiling my fun, so I entice Rhett inside the big house to get tongues wagging, although all I really want is to check out the home's décor, not his, and get some DIY tips from the workhands that I can take back with me to the 21st century.

Before this could be established, the director is now calling in his marker. Thousands of wounded and dying soldiers are pouring into Atlanta and I have been paired up with Mel, 'dear' Mel (quick, someone get me the sick bucket) to help out as they are being dumped on my doorstep.

God, it is like being at work. I applaud how extremely disorganised she is and yet do not applaud how sub-standard the conditions are out here. Seems a lesson or two in Universal Precautions wouldn't go amiss, although I have no time to think about these things right now.

These poor babies, their wounds are doomed never to heal without proper sterile dressings (if I had known I would have raided my old district nurses' supply) and I fear more amputations may follow. I cannot cope with this. I only came here to check out the landscape and I have a good enough idea of what it is inside Twelve Oaks to be able to recreate that in my 'dolls' house.' I only hope I can manage to find twelve of the same oak trees on eBay that I can stand around my field of creation.

Methinks it is time to abandon my post and go home, but not until I have said goodbye to Rhett. However my hands are all bloodstained, even through my powered-latex gloves, so I must wash them first.

I shall miss Prissy, my maid, the most. If I could take her back with me I would, and I would get her a job at my place. As a carer she would get paid for helping people to wash and get dressed, so she would not have to skivvy for free. I would be a kind boss to her – not a slave driver. It seems no one in Georgia has even heard of the Human Rights Act let alone practiced it.

Seems I won't get the chance to say goodbye to Rhett after all as he is running late on the battlefield, but I needed to get home so I have texted him instead now that I am back home.

OK, I have never owned a cotton plantation, but we did live in Sevenoaks at one stage of Hubby's career.

With not even a quarter of an acre of land, my little back garden was definitely not worth fighting for or dying for and it was definitely not the only thing that mattered back then. A spoilt beauty I am not, but as for having hovering demons ... hmm – that is debatable!

I may not get a standing ovation at the Academy Awards, but at least they appreciate me at work and maybe we will take on an Ashley lookalike one day, but this had indeed been a Reel Classic adventure for me and knowing that I had taken part, albeit briefly, in a film that was to spawn several decades was a real honour.

It is unlikely that Hubby should ever go rummaging around my wardrobe and notice the heavy green velvet dress hanging up which ordinarily one could not get off the peg. But in bringing it back with me on the QT the 'big house' had not been burgled (Rhett had let me in), I couldn't steal something that already belonged to me (I was Scarlett after all) and it was not daylight robbery – as I stuffed it into my suitcase in the middle of the night I did not hold a gun to my own head. I knew the difference between law and lust!

Next stop Emerald City. I had been told it was built of green glass and covered in emeralds and jewels, but I need to see for myself.

It would be safer to use green Perspex on the walls I think in my recreating and I will most definitely have trouble with the other things, since much of the jewellery my mother-in-law has sent me over the years have been from a well-known 'bid-up' channel on a late-night TV programme is a bit tacky; no offence Mum, but it is just not right for this job.

I told work I would not be in this Tuesday. I told my boss that I had a bout of dysentery, forgetting I was no longer part of a civil war, then, quickly pretending it was a deliberate mistake, I changed it to the 'runs'. I knew this meant that I could get away with not going in for the next 48 hours as policy rule, giving me the ideal time in which to complete my research of all houses great and small, yet I was only blagging one extra day off as Wednesday was my day off in any case.

That sorted, I reached for the remote control and pushed on the button that said 1939, and before I knew it I had landed slap bang in the middle of Dorothy's Travel Agents. The owner asked me why of all the travel agents in the whole of the county I had to walk into hers. I told her she ought to be grateful for the commission; that I could have blown my money going to check out the gin joints in Casablanca instead, but I could not see why it was any of her business why I wanted to travel along the Yellow Brick Road in any case.

She asked me if I would be travelling alone and I thought to myself, why on earth should I not? After all I do have a brain (a very sharp one at that), so I could always stop and ask a policeman if I got lost. I do have a heart (albeit a very loving if not a deep set one), which is why I am being so kind to her right now by not commenting on her awful dress sense. And I do have a lot of courage (I had risked getting shot at by both the Unions and Confederates, after all) so why on earth should I want to fork out for extra tickets for a bloke made of straw, a man made of tin and a lion with no roar to accompany me on my journey? What help could they possibly be?

My faithful travelling contraption has everything I need – a first-aid kit on board, a microwave oven and a 50" plasma TV, as well as internet access so I can google my way home if my satnav fails. But just as a precaution I have a telephone line installed that goes directly to my local police station and the blue light will flash on top if I get hijacked on my way to the Land of Oz. I have got everything covered.

As I move through the world of entertainment I have exchanged my uniform for a very fashionable blue and white chequered number and put my hair in pigtails. I still wear flat shoes, but these are red and nice and glittery.

I have landed at the end of the Yellow Brick Road and am full of excitement at finally being able to go in search of the great and powerful wizard, but there is a sign that says 'no access to cars'. I drag my machine into the forest for now, taking care to cover the tracks in the mud. But it is such a long and winding road (OK, you can stop singing now – another song that was made in a different era). It is too far for me to walk, and besides my ruby slippers don't have much tread left on them and it is quite slippery from all the rain they have had here recently.

As I close my eyes and wish I could magic my car

up, a taxi of a different colour pulls up. Great, I am thinking, but how am I going to be able to pay the cabbie?

Glinda (a good witch with a name badge) then appears from nowhere and whispers in my ear. I could swear she is chanting 'auntie M, auntie M', but in fact she is telling me where the nearest ATM machine is so I can swap my GBP for Oz gold. This is cool, I am thinking – just like putting a pound into a change machine on the pier at Weston-Super-Mud in exchange for tokens for the penny arcade.

The more we are following the rainbow left by the rain, the further away we seem to be getting. We have just passed a load of ugly-looking midgets along the way. Bert and I, having now been dropped off, are confronted with an Irish leprechaun who tells me he has a secret pot of gold hidden at the end of the rainbow and that if I find it I will be made for life. I know I will have more chance of winning the Irish Lottery back home.

Yes, you heard right. Bert! For starters Toto is on location at Emmerdale Farm as a temporary substitute for Edna's dog, who is in quarantine, and besides with Hubby away how could I possibly have left him at home alone? He and Kevin would have got up to all sorts of tricks. What kind of irresponsible pet-owner would that have made me? But it is very hard to keep a tight rein on my not-so-little pooch. He is extremely heavy and even if I were to find a bike with a basket on the front, it would never accommodate him. The hardest thing of all is trying to stop him from wanting to pee up against the spare yellow bricks we are encountering along the way.

Everything around me is surreal and to top it all, having pushed on the door of the Emerald Palace, which is slightly ajar, I find a grey-haired old man sitting in front of a voice activation machine (sounding very much like Sean Connery), so my spirits have been dampened even more than my hair.

Outside, the world is a magical place, but inside there is little that I would want to recreate back home, decoratively speaking. It won't stop me wanting to search out a miniature church organ though, just in case I change my mind.

By chance I have found a magic wand at the side of the road, and when I close my eyes and wave it around me and Bert it creates a tornado that pushes us back down the road and into the forest where the time machine is still sitting. I land right back in the garden, relieved to be home. I checked out the décor of the Emerald City, so job done. Now Bert will not have to pee outside his own backyard and I shall have no need to go looking for my heart's desire miniature wallpaper in any of the stores, because it was never there in the Green Palace in the first place!

I feel there is no real need for me to visit the Chocolate Factory next. I am most intolerant of naughty children and the Oompa Loompas really freak me out. I understand most DIY stores have run out of lickable wallpaper, but I could always paint over my own with coloured sherbet. Edible mushrooms I can frequently find in the bargain basement chilled compartment and there is an abundance of chocolate out there, although, given the limited space with which I must work, I may have to settle for a chocolate pond rather than a river.

That really just leaves the fourth section unaccounted for, but there is no rush. The 'house' is still in the box in the garage, having been there a while, so maybe it is already a luxury mouse pad. Not only that, I need Hubby to lug it all the way upstairs to the spare room before I can even begin to transform it into my dream house. With the help of my customised remote control I was able to go from Scarlett to Dotty in a matter of seconds, but there really is no place like home, and boy I am glad to be back. I fancy anything but salt pork or hardtack for tea!

MAD DATE 8

COME WHINE WITH ME

Wherever I have travelled so far, I have always been mindful that I needed to be home before tea. No one could have accused my siblings and me of being 'latchkey' kids. Mum and Dad knew at all times where each of us was, and that was never far away from Mum's apron strings. Even on non-school days we would not stray too far away – generally playing in the woods (for my brothers it was cowboys and Indians), while for us girls it was seeking out some new adventure to take back to Brown Owl.

As the eldest however, I was quite independent and Brownies taught me the art of self-reliance from a very early age, starting with learning how to tie that yellow tie that accompanied my milk chocolate brown uniform.

As I moved through secondary school I took up Home Economics, which was not simply about learning how to cook and serve up delicious 'nosh', it also encompassed other life skills, from first aid to personal finance and safety plans for a nuclear attack. Is it coincidence then that I am now competent at basic life support, sort out all the household bills each month and can understand very well how police emergency contingency plans work, even if I am only typing them up for his lordship?

Here today is a woman who grew up on stews and 'patties' made from leftovers from Sunday dinner – dishes that my dad used to make after he had slept off the couple of whiskies he had drank down in the Woodman in Highgate before coming home and insisting on being the one to serve up the meal, while Mum helped.

Those patties were to die for. They were definitely worth fighting my siblings for, and expecting them every week really did matter. I have tried to perfect my own attempts over the years but have never quite got it right. I spent a great deal of time watching dad cook. He never used a recipe yet churned out the tastiest and most economical meals for our brood that you could ever imagine. Mum did the bulk of the cooking. She was not quite so adventurous, but she was a real expert at 'bubble and squeak', and my brothers could not get enough of it.

One Easter, Brown Owl asked us girls to make an Easter bonnet for the fair. I made a pastry hat that was so hard she actually had to take a hammer to it, and at school I made a soufflé that was so light most of it ended up on the roof of the oven. My stick-jaw toffee was a dentist's delight – but I did make a mean flapjack!

Over the years my halo has somewhat dropped on the kitchen goddess front. My egg timer boils eggs to the point of explosion, as I forget they only need three minutes, and the royal icing on my Christmas cakes is not as regal as it used to be and certainly not as good as dad's used to be.

Hubby jibes me that if he ever came home and smelt a delicious meal in the oven then he knew he had gone to the wrong house. But I take in my stride his male chauvinistic remarks, which never offend me (like 'a woman's outlook on life should be through the kitchen window' or 'the reason why women have small feet is so they can get closer to the kitchen sink') and thankfully I have not quite spoiled a meal to the point where it cannot be saved.

As an ordinary housewife therefore, confined primarily to the daily grind of cooking, I make no apologies for my place in society as chief cook and bottle washer. I grew up watching Fanny and Johnny Cradock cooking on the TV in the afternoons and then the Galloping Gourmet, Graham Kerr, who always had a glass of wine in hand.

As the lamb stew (Hubby's all-time favourite) is simmering nicely away in the oven my own creative juices are continuing to work away behind my laptop, but I do not have long to 'prep' before it is time to serve it up, so apologies in advance if my imagination, on this occasion, might appear a little 'undercooked.' I am not downing large quantities of wine during the process – just the one, and sipping it slowly.

'If music be the food of love then play on' I am thinking as I drool over one or two of those celebrity chefs that grace today's TV screens. 'Give me excess of Gino di Campo, James Martin and Gary Rhodes that thine appetite may not sicken and die...' (this is me versus Shakespeare).

'Come dine with me, let's dine, let's dine away/If I could drink some exotic booze in that bar in far Bombay... ' (this is me versus Sinatra).

'Order for Hannibal Lecter ... a large helping of fava beans and a glass of Chianti and don't f*** up the menu or he'll eat me alive!' shouts Gordon Ramsay to the chefs – the man who is more meatballs than footballs these days, yet is still on a nice little earner.

The idea of my three favourite chefs actually jumping out of the TV right now and coming to my home would be a fairytale come true – a magical, mystical happening that will never occur. Talking of fairy tales, I am wondering which of them would make the porridge too hot, which too cold and which just right. Could Snow White resist biting into the Granny Smith apple that the lovely Gino offers her at the risk of becoming intoxicated as he eggs her on using his sultry brown eyes to seduce her?

This Cinderella wonders if James Martin would stick around long enough after shooting another episode of *Saturday Morning Kitchen*, or would he prefer the pumpkin on his worktop to turn into another Aston Martin rather than a glass coach?

They each tell tales of what their grandmothers used to make, which is very endearing, and my grandchildren are already raving about Nanny's cheesy mash, so maybe in years to come I too may get a mention if they ever decide to make the big time.

As I get carried away here, the 'D' word is coming to mind. Am I really going crazy? D, D, D – what does it mean? I've got it – dumplings! It's time to put the dumplings into the stew. Phew, what a relief. It could have been the other scenario, and I have not finished my book yet.

Right, so I have about ten minutes to finish stirring my imagination also. I have strayed away from the world of Hollywood and TV slightly, but my thinking cap is back on.

'Alice always took a great interest in questions of eating and drinking.' I have always taken more than an interest in both. Having my own family around for Sunday dinner is always a bit like a mad hatter's tea party at times. Hubby assumes his position at the head of the table (vitally important), elbows on the table are strictly forbidden, and it is important that everyone takes their designated seats and that the meal is served up in a very orderly fashion. All liquids and 'eats' are readily identifiable and thank goodness hubby has a Rolex, else he might be tempted to put butter into the clockwork of his grandfather's half-hunter pocket watch.

If anyone is allowed to fall asleep at the table it is him, and invariably it falls upon me to play mother and pour the tea afterwards. We are all quite bonkers in one way or another you know, but then all the best people are, aren't they? The writer Vivian Greene once said that 'life is not about waiting for the storm to pass but about learning to dance in the rain.'

OK, so I do not have a dishwasher and the kitchen looks like a bomb has hit it by the time we are generally finished, but I have learned to wash up exceptionally well over the years, just as my mother continues to do, and she taught me well, so what the heck!

There are always plenty of 'Drink Mes' and 'Eat Mes' left over and hubby and I look forward to a second sitting later in the evening when everyone has gone home.

In true movie fashion, if I were ever to open up my home for the cameras to compete for the £1,000 prize on Channel 4's *Come Whine With Me*, sorry I mean *Come Dine With Me* (see, one glass and I am confused), I should like to play the part of the director as well as the main actor. I would have no need for an assistant director, as I am quite capable of taking my guests' coats on arrival and handing out hors d'oeuvres, or horses hooves as Hubby calls them.

The cast would have to be carefully chosen. I should enrol friends who can provide a good dialogue to make interesting viewing, and if I keep topping up their glasses before they get anywhere near empty, then who knows what interesting revelations might emerge.

As for the set, my kitchen would be the stage, and as chef I must make sure to plan the menu.

Hollywood could meet Bollywood for one night only as my red-carpeted dining room turned into an Indian restaurant. A little background music, subdued lighting and candles would add to the ambience, and if the curry does not come out as well as it looks in the cookbook then this could hide a multitude of sins as I go from oven to table.

So what of the plot? There would be no hidden plan. The chance to have my guests enjoy my culinary skills on display for the whole TV world to see would be accomplished, provided no one falls off my bar stools, and the climax would be that we get to share the winning prize with each other. My guests would be ones that I could be assured would leave at a decent hour, as I am not very subtle when it comes to yawning and stretching and I should not want the viewers to consider me rude.

Perhaps one day I might even hold a *Gone With The Wind*-themed party for them, one that would evoke thoughts of warm summer nights, elegant southern mansions, cool iced drinks and fanciful 'southern' food (southern fried chicken maybe). But for now I must settle for the English rain outside and my little house in the not-so-deep south west and serve up the stew pronto before he thinks his throat has been cut, else it will be a right hullabaloo.

And talking of food, you may well have come to the conclusion that I am a few fries short of a Happy Meal, a few slices short of a loaf or even twenty shillings short of a pound, but hey, if this has not put you off just yet, keep reading. I am only just getting warmed up!

MAD DATE 9

VIRTUAL ROMANCE

Mae West, that platinum blonde from the silver screen, would joke, 'in Hollywood they got married early in the morning. That way, if it didn't work out they would not have wasted the whole day.'

I got married pretty early in the morning, but it did work out and the only thing that had been wasted (although not often) was me, after one too many Snowballs.

Similarly Groucho, one of the famous Marx brothers, has joked that 'in Hollywood the brides tend to keep the bouquet and throw away the groom'. I still have the bouquet and I still have the groom and the only thing I throw away is his left-over Chinese meals.

Whilst I am bemused by the cynicism of the stars, just like humour, romance is in the eye of the beholder, and we all know it comes wrapped in many different packages. Some might consider a marriage certificate to be a work permit for the woman and a guaranteed way for a man to get his ironing done for free, but I like to hold onto the notion that true love cannot be found where it does not truly exist.

My wedding certificate is my most prized possession, and whilst my not-so-cranelike legs are being worn into the ground in not-so-high-heeled shoes these days, I am completely comfortable with it, but the expectations of palpable chemistry, not too many odds for the lovers to overcome and preferably no devastating death scenes, remains high on my list of priorities when it comes to watching the old romantic movies.

As a young woman I was always drawn towards romantic tales on board cruise ships and was gutted to learn that Dr Adams and his crew are no longer taking bookings to sail to Fantasy Island, as the *Pacific Princess* has ceased trading.

Well, that's me out of the running for a stand-in job as Mr Rourke's (the Island's host) midget assistant. OK so I would only have operated from a bell-tower and my job would have been little more than to announce when 'de planes, de planes' of holidaymakers were about to land, but at least I would finally have had my own office.

What I want to know though is how can a whole tropical island just disappear from the Thomas Cook brochures without explanation?

Having reconciled myself to the fact that I must operate from my not-so-tropical surroundings, I recall my first encounter with the ocean on my first-ever holiday with my best friend and her family as we sailed from Brindisi to Patras on a camping holiday. I fell instantly in love with the captain of the MS *Appia* of the Hellenic Mediterranean and Adriatic Line. His name was Franco (original or what?) and the only thing hellish was that I was only 16 and not in a position to do anything about it. Hey Franco, I am older now. If you are out there still, look me up!

Five thousand nautical miles away from Tower Hamlets lived the man Mum eventually got to marry. As a merchant seaman travelling between Calcutta and Liverpool during the days of the British Raj, he had served on several merchant ships of the British Navy – those that which had kept our country supplied with arms, ammunition, food, fuel and other items needed during time of war. As the youngest of all the merchant seamen, dad signed on in 1946, given a 'Boy' rating holding the rank of 'Cabin Boy' and by the time he came out, having had a succession of voyages on what were termed the 'Empire Ships' because they were used during World War Two by the Ministry of Transport, he had worked his way up to a top-grade helmsman. His letter of recommendation from the owner of Thos & Jno Brocklebank Ltd – a famous line of Calcutta steamers – is a little worse for wear these days, but it's another valued possession I have inherited.

Mum and Dad's romance continued while he was at sea, and just as hubby had wanted me to leave the TA when he fell instantly in love with me, so too Mum was not prepared to be the wife of a seaman, so Dad gave up the navy without hesitation – lucky for me, else this story could be a whole new ball game.

Dad was not a religious man per se but he was a Roman Catholic, having been brought up by the nuns in a boarding school, primarily a privilege of the rich. He did not fall into that category but his teachers were far from sisters of mercy, as he would tell tales of getting the strap and of the ruthless regime which was his prescription for care. If anything good was to have come of that, they at least taught him discipline and gave him a good education, both of which have been handed down from generation to generation.

In comparison with my father, my grandmother was a staunch Catholic – the hospital in which she had nursed my granddad was run by Mother Theresa. Dad always used to say 'you'll never find a poor priest.' If only he had been alive when she died with the surrounding controversy over her misuse of funds, he would have told me 'I rest my case.'

As a child growing up, Nan swore by the holy water that she claimed came from a friend who had visited Lourdes and whenever I got ill, out it would come as she anointed me on the forehead. Funnily enough, it seemed to work. I got better very quickly. She had us believe it could fix anything.

I was far from brainwashed, but I did watch *The Song of Bernadette* many times with Mum and Dad and became mesmerised by Jennifer Jones' portrayal of the peasant girl who became a saint. Yet, whilst I was at a very impressionable age and cynicism was not in my DNA back then, I am far from holier than thou. Nan was called Mary but that was the only similarity – a virgin evidently not.

Just as the water at Lourdes continues to flow from a spring in the rock caves of the Grotto of Massabielle, Del Trotter's also came from a spring concealed by rocks, except it was connected to a nearby tap (*Only Fools and Horses*, 11th Christmas Special) and even if Nan had managed to pull the wool over my eyes all those years ago, after watching this with Dad, I learned never to take things at face value.

'Mother Nature's Son' was the name of the episode. My father was his mother's son and at the risk of being blasphemous, in his own jovial way I am sure he would have bucked up the courage to tell her that the water from the River Ganges would have served us kids equally as well if only she had 'believed'.

How easily I can go from Theresa to Trotter in a matter of seconds, but I am no ordinary girl as you can see. Memories of my dad have far from faded, even if photographs of him are looking a little battered these days. This is why it is important for me to reminisce so nostalgically about a generation gone by before everything fades into oblivion.

Talking of 'back home', I bought my mum a book by the same name – a story which was later turned into a film and starred a very young Hayley Mills. Whilst the settings and the storyline were somewhat different, the theme was the same, and I know she enjoyed reading it and thinking how lucky she was to have lived through such an historic event and found someone who could understand where she was coming from, having been a war child himself. Palpable chemistry they had. They had come through everything to survive the war, and the only devastating love scene for them was the one where Mum had to sit and watch Dad die, leaving her a widow at the age of 52. It was not a stage production or a dress rehearsal but real life. The only dress rehearsal was when Dad would let me wear his navy tunic, which was like a dress on me. I could pretend I was in some faraway place, just like Robinson Crusoe.

DON'T CALL ME CAMILLE

Perhaps now, people, you can appreciate why I see romance and the sea as one and the same.

'*We sometimes encounter people, even perfect strangers, who begin to interest us at first sight, somehow suddenly, all at once, before a word has been spoken.*'
(Fyodor Dostoesky, Russian novelist, 1821-1881).

So when I watched *Now Voyager* for the very first time, Bette Davis became my all-time favourite actress.

Now into our 34th year of marriage, it looks as if I shall never get to experience the romance of the seas, as Hubby's idea of a holiday is going to places of 'historic value', although he did talk about one of his officers having gone on a cruise only the other day and how fantastic the holiday snaps looked. But I cannot wait in hope of what might be, and I am impatient by nature.

It is Wednesday and I want to go right now, but I cannot cover the ocean in a day. Work is pretty manic these days and I do have a little annual leave left to take. Having cleared it with the boss, I have booked myself into a mountain retreat as a little respite from all the recent pressures. I have met this wonderful doctor who looks and talks like Claude Rains. He has given me a lot of his time and attention and 'crucial building up of my self-esteem'. I am neither depressed, highly-strung nor on the verge of a nervous breakdown just yet, but I have been a little 'edgy', and the doc has recommended a little convalescent trip on board an ocean liner.

Before I set sail for South America I must attempt to transform myself from an unglamorous mouse into one who might be considered vaguely beautiful, and I need to brush up on my assertiveness skills. First I must do away with the un-chic shoes and my sexless uniform and try to manage without my reading glasses. I have seen some wonderful high-heeled two-tone shoes in Asda as well as a very wide brimmed hat, so will hurry out and buy them before the sale ends.

Standing here in a very classy outfit that I have found at River Island, elbow-length gloves, stockinged legs and carrying the Louis Vuitton handbag I got from a Turkish market many years ago, I peer under the hat and catch a glimpse of my own reflection in the ship's window, contemplating the mystery of the transformation. I am turning the heads of every male passenger already. If only 'Franco' could see me now. I feel a little awkward in company, but do not want to appear too aloof.

I no longer have to hide those forbidden cigarettes from Hubby (34 years is a long time to have kept my secret smoking from him) as I smoke openly and elegantly from a very expensive cigarette holder that I bought online. Fear of identity fraud on the internet taught me one thing, if nothing else –never to reveal one's true self. So when I found myself being introduced to a stranger on the ship I was wary. How can I be sure his name was really Jerry, I was thinking, because he has a remarkable resemblance to Paul Henreid?

As the tides rolled by and we got to know each other better, he was keen to give me a nickname. He decided to call me Camille, because he said I reminded him of a camellia. Very quickly I asked Jerry if he would mind awfully calling me Camomile because I was English after all, not an American, and because whilst Hubby did not object to me popping in and out of film sets, he always insisted I was back in time for tea.

Plato was right – love is a 'serious mental illness' – and I for one need my head examined. Having let Jerry woo me, it turns out he is married and worse still I have learned he is only looking for a surrogate mother for his daughter Tina, an ugly duckling who wants me to turn her into a swan. God, it's a lot easier doing the drug round!

So the cruise did me little good really, but it got me out of the house for a while and I was glad to be back in uniform tending to others who were also needy, even if I am no longer an attractive figure of social grace and appeal.

Jerry loved me, I know he did, but he only gave me the stars and not the moon. Hubby would if he could afford it, and besides I am not sure I could play the part of the little wifey better for anyone else.

I was obsessed with Bette Davis movies from then on. Fancy a sneak preview at how I got on playing her in her other movies? First I assumed the role of Judith Traherne, a young socialite who fell in love with Dr Frederick Steele (aka George Brent) only to have him diagnose me with an inoperable brain tumour. However he told me he would help me die 'with dignity.' My last words to him were, 'Nothing can hurt us now. What we have cannot be destroyed. That's our victory – our victory over the dark. It is a dark victory (film of the same name) because we are not afraid.'

Great speech, but it did not help me to keep my man and let's face it, there is no good way to die now, is there?

As a headstrong southern belle from Louisiana in 1852 I earned the title of Jezebel, which caused me to lose my fiancé (aka Henry Fonda) as I was stubborn, vain and too proud to admit when I was wrong (now that rings a bell!) I tried my utmost to win him back, to no avail. I tried my best to be a good wife to a rubber plantation administrator, but could not resist the temptation to have an affair with a married man. In my character role of Leslie Crosbie, my poise, graciousness and stoicism impressed nearly everyone I met in Singapore, but when I claimed I had shot Herbert Marshall in self-defence, his interfering wife was trying to blackmail me over the letter I had written him asking him to meet me earlier on that day. With all my heart I still loved the man I killed, but it was too late to say sorry. Another one that got away!

Then there was Clem, dear Clem – my cousin's husband (George Brent once more) with whom I had had an affair and who, in a fit of anger, decided to join the battle of Vicksburg. He died before he could marry me, leaving me pregnant with his child that was later taken away from me. The child knew me only as Aunt Charlotte for years until the truth came out. Yet still I remained an old maid with a love-starved soul.

I was relieved when I got to play a Fanny instead of a Charlotte (it must have been the 'in' movie name between 1938 and 1932). I was beautiful and very popular, but my stupid brother Tippy tried to embezzle his employer, Mr Skeffington, out of much of his money. To try and get him off the hook, I had to woo him with the intention of marrying him. But then Tippy decided to go to war. He got killed and I was forced to live in a loveless marriage with a man who was so nice to me it made me feel sick.

As Mrs Skeffington I took a host of lovers after that, but none of them really loved me as Job did. My appearance was ravaged after I caught diphtheria, but as luck would have it he ended up blind so he could not see how old I was looking. Yet of all the people I was popping in and out of love with, he was the kindest of all. He always used to say 'a woman is beautiful only when she is loved.'

Having survived Guillain Barré syndrome back in 2002, my face and appearance had taken on a radical change, but Hubby stood by me, loved me in spite of it, and thankfully I have returned to 'normal' – if my readers could ever consider me to be normal after all this twaddle.

But I cannot drift into a daydream without finishing the end properly. In none of my acting roles did I want to lose touch with any of those men I had encountered or the actors that played them, so after all my relationships went pear-shaped I gave them the link to get onto my Disgracebook page. The application which I created was quite apt, I felt as they had each treated me disgracefully, and besides I needed to be mindful of copyright.

So in real life I have not signed up to social networking, but that does not mean I have not had my fair share of penfriends in the past. Mind you, I am going back a bit. Postal mail (or snail mail as it is now called by comparison), was so much more fun, but then life in the 70s was a lot simpler and safer. For anyone who can remember, as I do, those loved-up teenage magazines like *Oh Boy, Blue Jeans, Jackie* and *Loving* will recall that it was not uncommon to find real photographs of people who were looking for a penfriend, home or abroad, even having their home addresses printed next to them. There was nothing covert about it, though it's a little scary to think what might happen these days if you didn't write back quickly enough.

Still, whilst my not-quite-so-arthritic fingers are still holding out, I prefer to pick up the corded telephone (mobile if I must) and hold a proper conversation that does not include me having to 'decipher' text language which I absolutely H8!

All I can say is IM50+, GMAB. I am fifty plus, give me a break!

'Friendship is born at the moment when one person says to another, 'What! You too? I thought I was the only one.' (C.S. Lewis, 1898-1963)

Here's to being able to still write to people in my own age group with similar hobbies and interests upon which a good pen-pal relationship is based.

THE ESSENCE OF TIME

Would you be very shocked if I were to pour myself a small Martini? It's awfully early, I know, but it must be six o'clock somewhere in the world. Actually it was Audrey Hepburn who said that, in her book *How to be Lovely*, but she was referring to a small whisky, so I am adapting it here to match my own tastes. I hope you are not a little 'shaken' by this.

I shall be very careful not to spill a drop while I am strolling along on Moonlight Bay, as Gordon McCrae waits for me to cuddle up a little closer under the light of the silvery moon.

I can't stay there long though, as Trevor Howard is waiting for me at the railway station – waiting for me to wave goodbye to him after our affair as a result of a very Brief Encounter has come to an end.

As I quietly contemplate where I have travelled in my movie mind, I have indeed been around in more ways than one. I have walked along Waterloo Bridge dressed as a prostitute instead of a ballerina, but should not have done so if I had known that Roy was still alive, having met him during an air raid having had to go to war soon after. If I had only thought about changing my name to Holly Golightly I might have had someone treat me to Breakfast at Tiffany's.

I have spent endless days sitting in a café in Casablanca with Sam reminding me that 'a kiss is just a kiss and a sigh is just a sigh' and wishing that Rick would wear some other suit.

I have been to Australia, where I wasted no end of time pining for a priest, but Father Ralph just would not relent and break his vows for me. My mother in law, incidentally, once told me Hubby wanted to be a priest, yet he went on to become 'an officer of de law'. Still, I guess he still got to wear a black uniform.

And, I have also been to the Yorkshire Dales, by gum, where I stood patiently waiting for Daddy, my Daddy, to emerge from a cloud of smoke having been cleared of all charges of selling state secrets to the Russians. So, if anyone were to ask me whether I would consider living a Hollywood way of life as opposed to my own – living in magnificent mansions, enjoying a cascade of luxuries, going to endless cocktail parties and having a series of romantic rendezvous –

in my make-believe world the answer would have to be YES.

To date I have been like a stealth butterfly suspended effortlessly in a makeshift sky, my wings been beating very, very fast to keep up with all my fantastical adventures. If a picture paints a thousand words, I hope that by now you will have a rough sketch of what makes me who I am today. Alas, I shall never be one to personify Hollywood glamour – only in my world of make-believe where I have had the privilege of passing through the gates of my dream factory.

When it comes to glamour I have two trains of thought. As a movie star should I go 'all out' and live in an aura of that glamour or should I assume a screen role of the 'girl next door' where glamour is saved for the performance itself?

But then I got to thinking, what would be so wrong with just being me? So I am getting on a bit, but it has been said that the best wine comes out of an old vessel and that a good broth may be made in an old pot.

If I were looking for a date, which I am not, what else might you like to know about me? Perhaps you might like to conjure up whether I smell as good as I look – but hey, how do I look? I have had many different facelifts and personality changes here.

'Perfume is like a piece of clothing, a message, a way of presenting oneself, a costume that differs according to the woman who wears it.' – Paloma Picasso, French fashion designer.

Just as the smell of a favourite dish brings back memories of cooked meals at home, so too the scent of many a good perfume has helped to cement my memories of love, romance and plain old-fashioned friendships in my own life and that of others dear to me.

I recall my mum's all-time favourite, Evening in Paris, one of the most celebrated perfumes throughout the world – a firm favourite during World War II, although she would have been too young to have worn it then. It has since been re-launched as Soir de Paris (a simple translation, yet it sounds so much more romantic). It was a fragrance that claimed to evoke romance when worn, and it evidently worked while she was courting my dad.

It is a shame her sense of smell has somewhat diminished over the years, as no doubt a little spray on her wrist would be enough to recall those days when she was young and carefree.

I have the perfume giants Houbigant, Fabergé, Coty and Nina Ricci to thank for titillating my 'taste buds' as a young woman. Although I did not get paid much in the day, it did not deter me from spoiling myself with the likes of Chantilly, Blasé, Kiku and Green Apples. Alas, they are now as 'vintage' as I am, but the smells (unlike me) are fresh as a daisy in my mind. Hey, hasn't someone since brought one out under that name?

As I have matured, so too has my desire to 'smell the part'. In true movie fashion, I should like to go out in Shakespearean style wearing any one of the following with a written statement to go to whatever love interest I am scripted in with at the time:

Poison (by Dior) (Original)

'Romeo, Romeo, wherefore are thou bottle of Poison that I may sprinkle it upon my person with no need for consumption, that I shall be consumed only with passion till the end through its sweet aroma...'

L'Eau d'Issey (By Issey Miyake)

'That my soldier boy and I should have the 'his' and 'her' versions to allow us to be joined together in Holy Perfumery against the backdrop of a coppy-woppy and nursey-wursey relationship; That I shall once more be able to perform as a Kabuki dancer for my lovely GI; That we will never again have to say 'Sayonara.'

AP Matrisse (by Agent Provocateur)

'That I may endure the sweet smell of success as an eternal seductress, that allows this eau de parfum with its passionate 'whiff' of white lotus petals and delicate white Ylang Ylang, to hypnotise my lovers so that they will never leave my sight again.'

Maybe I should bring out my own version of Liebfraumilch. A quick dab of it behind the ears and hey presto I might even 'pull' at the next alcoholics anonymous meeting!

MAD DATE 12

THE FINAL FRONTIER

It is said that butterflies typically only live for a few months, maybe a little longer, and are sent to remind us to make the most of the here and now. If you were to ask me today the same question about living the Hollywood dream, the answer would be different.

'We have all the time in the world' according to Louis Armstrong when singing the title of a 1969 James Bond theme (that date, somewhat ironic don't you think?)

'He has all the time in the world' – those famous last words of the film upon which much of my fantasy first evolved.

But what if none of these worlds ring true and

what if there are some things Nan's holy water just cannot fix?

'Home is a place not only of strong affection but of entire unreserved; it is life's undress, its backroom, its dressing room.' – Harriet Beecher Stowe, (1811-1896).

Neither my sense of humour nor my sense of smell have diminished since my last 'mad date' and writing in the way that I am about to do now gives me the legitimacy to be able to come out of that 'backroom' in which I have been hiding for almost half a decade; events during that time that I could never have rehearsed and where scripts lay hidden that the world chooses to ignore. I can smell a rat a mile away and whilst all the fun and frolics of my mad dates so far are behind me, one thing is not – something I can only describe as a pantomime, in which the part where hope triumphs over adversity seems to have been left out. 'Oh yes it has, oh yes it has!'

It seems only right and proper that I should use the opening of a well-known police drama to get my literary juices back into action as I say to all you ladies and gentlemen out there 'the story you are about to hear is true. Only the names have been changed to protect the innocent.' (*Dragnet*, 1954)

Since the imaginary world that I recruited you into all those years ago involved me hopping in and out of my very own time machine, it seems only right that I should take you on my final journey in this way.

The topsy-turvy world that has since been bestowed upon me is evident in my writing as I flit in and out of different story books, yet I know no other way of being able to write the ending without landing myself in hot water.

His business was bullets, mine bandages, and it is time for me to 'wrap' things up for now. I am confident you will not need a degree with which to interpret it.

Having been parked up for so long, my faithful time machine needs a little WD40. I have no one to hide it from any more and it is right where I had left it.

As I brush away the cobwebs and brush my own self down, I am catapulted at the touch of the gear lever back to the year when the Mayans predicted the world would come to an end. Having been to Mexico six years before, Hubby and I had Great Expectations that we would live a lot longer than that. So fasten your seatbelts – it is going to be a much bumpier ride than before.

This time the years do not pass by in a matter of seconds. Instead I observe the changes that, unknown to me, are about to occur in my world in very slow motion. The traversing of the sun and moon in the sky has been replaced by black thunderclouds which are not bouncing back and forth like ping pong balls. The surroundings outside my machine are neither blurred nor faint, and every little detail is being etched on my brain. The endless models of smart phones and computer tablets with all their accessories sit in the store windows below me where the mannequins once stood to mark the changing time.

Sitting here under the flame from the LED candle in my vehicle which cannot help but remain alight, I am reminiscing about the time when I had the luxury of being an imaginary single, yet at the same time knew that there was always someone to put the kettle on for at the end of my working fantasy days. I am picturing, vividly, the day when winter was turning to spring when Hubby casually remarked that he had booked us on a cruise.

He had his football, I had my writing (my escapism), yet we had a telepathic connection after so long together. I mean, how else could he have known that I had been secretly tapping away on my keyboard about all those romantic sea adventures that only ever happened on screen and that in having mentioned his officer's photographs he was secretly sussing out my opinion on a cruising holiday? Good cop, clever cop!

In a month of Sunday dinners I could never have predicted that – no more than he could have predicted having to make a decision about early voluntary retirement from the Force after thirty-three non-recurring years in the same job.

The prospect of being able to get in some time to go fishing or put the finishing touches to his World War Two dioramas, however, was an enticement, even if the retirement package was less than inviting. Signing away his career was never going to be easy, but handing in his warrant card was going to be the hardest thing of all.

This was not going to be just any old cruise. It was an anniversary gift to ourselves; one that we both deserved, having only ever been allowed to hover among the 'monetary stars' but never quite being able to make an affordable moon landing. This was the nearest we were to come to a touch of class – a time to be able to put aside all the stresses that had led up to that moment which had brought out less favourable traits in us, yet, as always, we had managed to withstand the test of time.

How I would have loved, loved, loved to be able to let him have a sneak preview of the chapters in my book just then, so that he could have learned that he had made all my dreams come at once. I thought, finally I might get to play Camille, I mean Camomile, for real and spend my evenings lighting up his cigarettes for him while we had the Freedom of the Seas upon us. I would soon be on that pathway to the moon.

My joke about him being Scrooge only ever came out the Christmas before he retired, and the black furry Santa hat with white trim that flashed up 'Bah Humbug' still works to this day. I had bought it as a joke as the kids and I had noticed he had become very grumpy of late, not fully appreciative of the life-changing decisions he was being forced to consider in the year ahead.

As those black clouds hurry by, the engine management light is beginning to flicker and as I stare at it with concern, I am thinking now is not the time for it to break down. Suddenly everything has gone dark, yet there is a glimpse of light in the corner through which I am seeing silhouettes. I am standing at the altar in that lovely little church in Muswell Hill that stands not a stone's throw away from where I was born. I have taken a visionary detour back to one special day in October 1977 which changed my life forever.

The soft white gloves he wears by special permission of his Chief Constable complement well the white lace on the neckline of my dress and my netted veil as we stand there together side to side promising to spend the rest of our lives together – for better, for worse, in sickness and in health, till death do us part.

'What God hath joined together' quotes the priest with an obvious lisp, 'let no man put asunder.'

Jokingly whispering in my ear 'and this is about all it amounts to' he hands me a ten pence piece as 'all his worldly goods he doth thee endow'. That was something that would stay with us throughout our married life. He would sceptically say that we had two hopes of ever getting rich – no hope and Bob Hope. It was to be our Sod's Law that where one would giveth with one hand they would quickly taketh with the other, if we ever got a break.

I have now stepped the machine up a gear and fast-forwarded almost 34 years ahead to when we finally made it onto that luxury cruise liner. Hubby couldn't pull millions out of the retirement fund with those white gloves – he was not a rabbit after all – but he had picked out more than enough notes to flash around so that everyone could see that Mr and Mrs Upgrade had arrived from little old England.

Those two and a half weeks together were the best medicine we could have hoped for. It afforded us the chance to embrace the positive qualities in each other which often get forgotten over time, and despite a period of negativity in our lives for a very short while, we always knew we had each other's backs.

Home is where the heart is, and my heart was anywhere he was. Plus, I never did need a mountain that overlooked the sea, as anywhere he was with me was home. Cheers Elvis, for allowing me to be inspired by your work without breaching copyright!

So whilst we had sailed in relatively high fashion, and even though I did not get to wear that wide-brimmed hat, provide therapy on board to an ugly duckling teenager or light his fags for him, I for one was glad to get back to my more comfortable existence.

Our trip had been planned and the travel agents had simplified the process by coming up with the most appropriate package that took into account our individual needs. After the consultation session, we were confident that any important information that was needed by the reps at the end of our destination was fully documented so that we would be taken care of properly.

Having bulldozed Hubby into going to see the 'quack' a few weeks later, when he looked a bit peaky and was feeling out of sorts, the young doc (who was barely out of short trousers and bore a strange resemblance to one of the lollipop kids), had his own thoughts on why he may have appeared not to be firing on all cylinders, yet was keen to get a second opinion, having made no outward commitment to where he felt this might all lead.

It was as if I had written the doc's lines for him: 'I could work at a problem for years but to wait inactive for 24 hours was another matter'. We were grateful that a quick referral was made to his reps at the bigger airport not a few miles away. It was evident he did not want to be the one to 'decide whether or not this mere mortal's life would have meaning beyond the threshold of vital functions.' In this case, his vital signs – that is, blood pressure, pulse and general presentation – for those of you who are not familiar with the term.

It is fair to say I was still suffering from book overload at the time. Perhaps he could give me a prescription to download an app that might enlighten me as to how I could refrain from getting nearer and nearer to mercury poisoning, as the time it took for him to reach a decision was making me mad.

Had our Granada Scorpio not had a flat, I would have driven him there in 'normal style' instead having to listen to him and the time machine coughing and spluttering as we headed out in crazy fashion to our assigned destination. As I prayed that the moving parts in each case would carry on running freely, not start to stick or stop working altogether (until we got there), I could not help but think of Mum, who would have added 'as the actress said to the bishop' as she always did; Hubby always told me I had a screw loose on a regular basis.

My screws were perfectly intact, thank you, but the same could not be said of our flying companion as my gaze dropped downwards. Lo and behold, a small object went scampering across the floor – well, rolling to be precise. No, it was not a small snail this time but a butterfly screw. 'If it comes back it is yours, if it doesn't it never was' I was thinking, whilst recalling what he had told me his grandad had once told him about women and love. After we had hurriedly twisted the component back into place, top gear kicked in and before we knew it we found ourselves on a dinky little landing strip round the back of A&E. Anyone would have thought we were turning up in an open top helicopter with a pink pin-cushioned seat – but hey ho, the usual car park was full as usual in any case.

'I could murder that pint' he said, waiting patiently for evening to arrive so that no one could accuse him of drinking at an 'indecent' hour, but the only thing this 'watering hole' had waiting for him was an intravenous solution – 0.9% sodium chloride. He was only dehydrated after all. A quick blast of the old medicinal 'amber nectar' and all was destined to come good, had it not been for the referral letter that the lollipop kid had insisted we took with us.

How could we possibly have known that doc had documented Hubby to have been somewhere between dizzy and dead when ready for onward transmission? What lay behind those revolving doors did not suggest a luxury package was on offer, and he wondered if he could make a 'secret escape.'

Hubby had not hand-picked the accommodation and this was definitely not the type of service to tempt him away from home; it was a spontaneous booking made by the doc. As a player in a game of moans, I knew that at the throw of a medical dice there was a good prospect of hubby picking up an infected card by chance that would then entitle him to two lots of antibiotics – taking a further chance that they would be the right ones for the job. That would all be down to the medics of course, who had the monopoly on prescribing.

Having handed over the 'travel document' to the guy at the 'check-in desk' earlier – that which had been stamped and sealed by the medical midget – he and I were soon led away. Whilst it was considered to be a priority 'booking' there was little to suggest that a room reservation was needed beyond an hour or two.

So Hubby smoked cigarettes for over three decades (filtered, I might add, else as 'Camomile' I should never have attempted to light them up for him) and had chosen to drink alcoholic beverages without excuse on oh so many occasions over the years (to help numb the prospect of having to think too much about pressure of work and then premature retirement), but there was no excuse for the booking clerk or the 'concierge' to have surreptitiously been given unfiltered access to everything about my man's health since he cut his first teeth, as this meant his immediate problem was overlooked. During those critical seconds of reading, something could have been done about it.

Both the guy at the desk and the first medic he bleeped had failed to raise the medicinal sails that would have set him on the right course of treatment. Instead, though little did we know it, he was cruising towards many a bruising.

The clerk had asked not what time 'sir' might like an alarm call in the morning or what time he might expect that his bed be turned down before retiring, but seemed only to focus on his social habits. In having submitted much more information than was absolutely necessary, the lollipop kid had made it very easy for the 'crew' to be spared having to carry out an experimental search of the possibilities, instead settling for what might have seemed the obvious.

I was thinking, 'hey, why not ask me how many Babychams I have had over the past three decades?' At 6% alcohol by volume, they are more potent than anything he had drank out of a can (or put in a pint glass).

We were not there to justify the state of our livers. I was more intent on wanting to find out how they were going to save my beloved's bacon. So we were docked up on the assessment ward for the rest of that afternoon. It was on the fourth floor – the uppermost 'deck' – unlike the fifteen that we had ventured upon during our previous 'voyage' – we had explored them more than once, except for the Skylight Chapel.

This deck bore no resemblance to the Palace of Green Porcelain (thanks HG for allowing me the comparison), yet it housed many a 'passenger' in outdated green pyjamas, and Hubby was about to join their ranks.

'Looking around I saw white figures. Twice I fancied I saw a solitary white ape-like creature running rather quickly up a hill and once near the ruins I saw a leash of them carrying some dark body.' – The Time Machine, H.G. Wells (1866-1946)

Was I sharing in his lordship's state of dehydration, I wondered, sitting there by his bedside thinking such a bizarre thing, or was it just that for that split second I wished none of this was happening and that I was really back home jumping right back into my secret writing?

Afraid to tell any of the 'crew' that I needed a drink in case it got misinterpreted as evidence that I was alcohol dependent before I could get a chance to explain – a drop of the old H_2O was all I was after – it was important that I could justify, with some logic, what I had just witnessed before I was myself forced to have them bleep the mental health team and carry out an assessment of my state of mind.

Having taken a sip of Ribena from the small carton in front of him, I began to put things into perspective. I *had* seen white figures, but they were just ordinary doctors in white coats and only a trained eye would recognise that they were specialists. The solitary white ape-like creature running rather quickly 'up the hill' was a consultant who had not been blessed with the looks of Lauren Bacall (bless her), and the 'hill' was a wheelchair ramp strategically placed both sides of the ward entrance. As for the 'leash' thing – well it was, in fact, a group of medical students hurriedly carrying a politically correct resuscitating 'Andy' dummy towards the antiquated skills room.

Outcome of my own assessment – NOT mad as a hatter! No outward signs or symptoms of mercury poisoning just yet – not even a slight tremor on the Richter scale to suggest otherwise, and any mood swings I was having were attributed to the fact that the 'crew' seemed to show little concern for the welfare of their latest passenger, simply disappearing behind the privacy screens, never to return unless actively summoned. Hubby might have got a quicker response if he had resorted to using his police dog whistle, which for some strange reason he had not thought to bring along.

It was the Red Queen who eventually came back through the cotton-lined 'looking glass' (OK, medical registrar if you like), but it did not take long for the wordplay to begin. She was very good at thwarting my attempts at any logical discussion over the likelihood of Hubby's state of dehydration being down to simple heat exhaustion as the result of the tropical heat from previous days.

I wanted her to consider things from my perspective, but instead she was very bossy, gave us no helpful advice but instead muttered 'I don't know what you mean by your perspective, all the perspectives here (waving her unclenched hands around the deck) belong to me.'

What she was basically saying was that she was going to run the ship her way. Yes, your majesty, I was thinking – I am surprised you did not ask me to open my mouth a little wider when I spoke (*Through the Looking Glass*, Lewis Carroll 1832-1898).

A couple of rather portly gentlemen later appeared dressed the same. Maybe the mercury was beginning to take hold after all, as for that split second I was thinking 'which one is Tweedledum?' I could not resist asking one of them whether or not it was 'simply the heat of the day' that had forced hubby to be put in a bed. He turned to me and replied that it sounded 'plausible enough', but that we should wait until the next day – wait for the 'common sense of the morning' to kick in.

I would not have been surprised if the other doc was thinking 'in having to face this world, learn in ways and water it, this man and his wife ought to be careful not to hasten guesses as to meaning and that in the end they might find clues to it all.' Thanks HG – at least we knew where we stood, even if none of the Tweedledumasses made any sense. I hazard at a guess as to what my other half was thinking; that this was, indeed, little more than verbal diarrhoea.

My interpretation of what the Tweedles had said was that in stopping over, the specialist officers on board would have had more time to consider other possibilities for my man's acute illness and that the clues could then be found through proper diagnostic testing. That seemed like a good idea.

His overnight 'cabin' was neither spacious nor innovative. There was no sign of the Virgin Islands ahead, and even if there had been he did not have a sea view.

Running up a tab on the credit card really wasn't necessary – after all, he had been paying for this service for over 50 years without ever having 'cashed in' before now. Jokingly I told him to consider it as a post-holiday excursion where he could be looked after, as he had been by attentive 'stateroom attendants' at hand 24/7. He could still catch a movie or two on board, if I were to pop downstairs and buy him a TV and phone card from the vending machine in the foyer, which I did.

The unique four-digit phone extension number that would allow him to receive incoming calls without having to leave his bed was no substitute for the sea pass he had become accustomed to using, which had given us exclusive access to the cutting-edge adventures on our holiday, but it was better than nothing.

So what if he could not upgrade the linen, and would have to settle for a quick run under the communal shower tonight instead of a spa treatment? So what if the menu did not match that of Portofino's nor takes his palate around the world; at least the pre-packed sarnies would fill a gap and he would not have to get dressed up for dinner – the PJ dress code being casual and all that. And so what if his 'deck' was not technically advanced to the point where he could watch in awe as robots mixed him cocktails instead of having to settle for a cocktail of pills being served to him in a disposable 30ml pot by someone not in a grass skirt, having to settle for water to wash it down? After all, why should any of this have mattered? It was only going to be for one night and he would not have to 'rough it' for long. He guessed that asking for an ashtray and a pint at that point was out of the question.

Since there was to be no Cruise Compass delivered that evening – the daily guide our attendants used to bring us, which laid out what activities were available on our ship and what events were coming up, as well as the latest on weather on the Caribbean islands where we had been cruising previously – he would have to settle for the TV guide I had bought him so he could embark on a bit of channel hopping.

'Don't worry if you hear the sound of waves in your sleep', I told him, in case he thought he was delirious. 'It will be little more than the sound of the running taps nearby and the only link to anything remotely 'tropical' would be the palm-to-palm motion of the 'deckhands' carrying out the obligatory handwashing five-step technique'.

As for wanting to know the result of any activities that had taken place, such as his vital signs and any medical events that might be forthcoming, he only had to read the file at the end of his bed, although I knew he would leave this for me to do at my next visit as he was used to analysing crime files as opposed to medical.

With no cause for concern and having returned home, I rummaged through our old DVD collection until I came across *The Road to Bali*. Perhaps it was the 'no hope and Bob Hope' joke he used to make about going into hospital and getting out of there alive that made me seek it out after God knows how many years of gathering dust.

Sitting there laughing as Jane Russell emerged from a raffia basket at the sound of a flute made me forget for one second that Hubby was not actually outside in the garden having a cigarette and that he was not about to pop in and tell me that Bing was the lucky one and that he really was Bob because he had got me instead. If you haven't seen the film folks, I don't wish to elaborate and spoil the fun!

In the days that followed Hubby became little more than a human pin-cushion. Forget the butterfly wings of love and the butterfly-winged screw that had got us there in the first place, he had his very own butterfly needle in his arm from which endless blood was taken by all those who dared to have a stab at him. There were many candidates, it has to be said.

In the days that followed, if he could have sent me a postcard from every deck (ward) he had been transferred to in a bid to find out what was really wrong with him, I should have had a right good collection by the time it was over.

So whilst I had been sitting at home watching Bing and Bob doing a little 'island hopping', likewise his lordship had been doing the same as his health passport took him through the realms of the diagnostic department and several treatment 'cabins' before he ended right back on the special one from which he had already come – after he had become a real-life stand-in for that resuscitating Andy. Whoever said a ship in a harbour was safe needs shooting.

Had I insisted on taking him home with me that very first night, with the right treatment and my care we could have ridden the temporary storm together, and even if it had resulted in an unpredictable turbulent wave, at least he would have been shipwrecked at home, with me, where he belonged.

When the lollipop kid doc had forwarded him on, Hubby was little more than dripping wet, so how was it that he went from this to being soaked to death (in a manner of speaking) in such a short space of time?

He hated being there, especially all the poking and prodding, and even then, confident that things were going in the right direction (albeit with less insight than I had assumed), I would tell him to 'just go with the Flo.' In other words, to listen to me – the one who was in the business of repairing people and then shipping them out 'successfully.'

If there had been a Dr Emmett Brown at the helm on that fatal day, I could have bleeped him to arrange for some lightning to strike one of the clock towers in North London so that I could be whisked back to some seven hours before, when I had left Hubby alive and well. It has transpired that one or more of the crew members had failed to throw the love of my life the lifeline he needed, even though the red flags were signalling a disaster waiting to happen. It was like the *Titanic* all over again.

The kids and I needed answers.

'Our knowledge is very limited because nature is too shy and slow in our clumsy hands. Someday this will be better organised and still better. That is the drift of the current in spite of the Eddie's.'

I am not in the time machine now, I was thinking, as I urged the consultant and her team to stop talking nonsense such as this and tell it to us like it is. A classic interpretation of the works of HG at this point would have been that their knowledge of how Hubby had come to be ready for discharge one day and dead the next was indeed limited. Yet, I was thinking, it was your clumsy hands that allowed the diagnostic oversights to escalate his condition from an acute to a critical stage which, without the right treatment, had quickly led from slight chest pain to suffering a respiratory arrest from which he was put in an induced coma, intubated and given medication that sought to aggravate rather than repair, resulting in his eventual death. A death that could easily have been avoided had the care not been so fragmented.

Hubby's Sod's Law theory had finally rung true, and I had two hopes of getting a straight answer from them – no hope and Bob Hope. Just as had happened at Tara, I never got to say goodbye to my real-life Rhett, but this time it was not my hands that were bloodstained, metaphorically speaking.

'I think one's feelings waste themselves in words; they ought all to be distilled into action which brings results' – Florence Nightingale (1820-1910). I was about to put her theory to the test and get to the bottom of what really happened to the man I had loved and lost without warning – my world now turned upside down.

In putting my literary skills to the test I never set out to try to be smart or cool – witty maybe – and I am sure that if I were forced to take a blood test right now it would come back positive that I have a warped sense of humour, especially at a time like this. But then the events during that short admission had been a joke from start to finish.

Permission to liken myself to what the repercussions would be for the mighty oaks of Tara as the result of a full force tornado. I was feeling completely uprooted now that my real-life acting partner was no longer by my side,and if my face was Scarlett it was due to rage. Insult humour was not something I was about to tolerate as I set out on my own voyage of discovery at local level. I wanted to see if certain people who had chosen to remain faceless and nameless were confident enough to think that I, a mere public morsel, would sit back and take the brunt of their patronising and oh-so-not-funny comments about how this 'unfortunate event' had occurred, and that I should just accept it and do nothing about it.

Wrong! This particular 'nightingale' (with the badge to prove it) was about to sing in the political squares. In trying first to get answers at local level I found myself going through the looking glass as I entered a fantastical world of lies that to one cared to see beyond. A kaleidoscope of catastrophes lay buried at the bottom of the rabbit hole.

In moving around this nautical chessboard I first stumble across the 'dodo birds' seated within their 'advisory liaison' nests where the charmed life they lead means they need to do little more than take down a few 'particulars'. They have been well trained not to show any kind of sorrow, living only to serve the reptiles on their 'island' habitat. They have no need to worry about their natural defences being penetrated by less than amenable and dissatisfied complainants since all they have to do is to go back into hiding, or indeed disappear off the face of the earth, much like their counterparts of over three centuries ago, having forced the 'players' towards the Queen of Hearts – appointed to protect all those who reign under her with stethoscopes around their necks. The title of hospital manager may not sound as exciting and she may not swan around the place in a long white dress dotted with jam tarts, but nevertheless she did impress me by her ability to run at breathtaking speed away from any suggestions by me of foul play.

'Obstacles are like wild animals. They are cowards, but they will bluff you if they can. If they see you are afraid of them they are likely to spring upon you; but if you look them squarely in the eye, they will sink out of sight.' - Orison Swett Marden (1848-1924).

I was not about to humour them in their game of 'issue avoidance'. The intention to have me move further and further away from her, pushing me back towards her pawns (designed to do exactly what she expected of them and no more) was not going to work.

Just because I was not prepared to sit down with them over a cup of tea to find some 'resolution' does not mean that I was afraid of them. Looking them squarely in the eye would have only meant that my vulnerability would have shown and allowed them to spring upon me any old cock 'n' bull story.

I was not prepared to be bluffed, and I would keep them in my sights for as long as I could. For those who had been responsible for allowing my other half to have arrested in the first place, how could they have got away with fobbing me off so that they could then sleep peacefully in their beds at night – like the door mice in Wonderland? Besides, the rules had changed. I was now in Blunderland.

Whilst it may have taken me until I was 46 before I was able to 'sign up' to Flo's 1893 idealistic attitude that prevention is better than cure, that code of ethics is something which I have managed to establish and maintain over the years. I am in the business of treating people rather than a disease. I hope that when my time comes Dr Adams will look after me. We both have a wicked sense of humour, you see. We both 'look between the fingers' and the only difference between Patch and me is that when I bent down to receive my diploma I definitely had my frilly knickers on. (*Patch Adams*,1998.)

All hail Johnny Nash (1972), but the dark clouds have not gone and it has yet to be a bright, bright, sunshiny day. The rain has not stopped either, and the obstacles to justice are still in my way. I can see clearly now that I still have a long way to go.

'Ward cruises' showcased the very worst that was on offer during Hubby's trip and I urge all future 'passengers', voluntary or otherwise, to read the small print in the 'conditions of service'. There is a clause that suggests that any travellers who have, at any point in their lives, smoked or drunk 'over the odds' would automatically forego the opportunity to be diagnosed impartially, and to receive any treatment that could improve their quality of life or extend it in the event of any illness, related or not, and will be considered to be an unnecessary drain on the ship's resources.

Don't get too alarmed, folks – the service is available to others 'irrespectively' – even with an 'unconventional' marital status – where steps will definitely be taken to 'improve, prevent, diagnose and treat' both one's physical and mental problems with 'equal regard'.

I am sitting here thinking to myself, was it because he was not important enough that the seriousness of his illness was treated with such disregard? Should Plato, Socrates, Inspector Morse or the Man Called Ironside's excuses for drinking regularly without public scrutiny have been frowned upon, would they too have had the severity of their illnesses played down?

Likewise, I wondered, would Columbo, having turned up puffing away with a cigar in hand whilst complaining of being short of breath, or Mr Bean with a pipe in hand having swapped his idiotic ways for the part of a Parisian hero (aka Jules Maigret) in asking for antibiotics for a chest infection, have been given the benefit of the doubt that perhaps there was some other reason why they ought to put the tobacco back in the tin and get checked out?

The answer in the first instance is no; the second yes. In any normal real-life scenario of similar features, the average hard-working Joe might just as well go straight to the 'ice chamber'.

The ship's signposts are still as clear as day in my mind. There is Alice with drink in hand on the sign that reads and directs the 'passengers' to the new referral's non-alcoholic tea party; the one with

Tweedledum and Tweedledee in tuxedos that reads and directs them to the deck reserved exclusively for those who only indulge in 'clean living'; the one with a white rabbit on, cane under arm, that asks the passengers to 'follow the consultant'; a sign at the entry of all decks bearing a cartoon of the Mad Hatter that reads 'We're all sick here'; and the most widely-recognised sign of all, where the Red Queen is pointing out that the morgue is 'that-a-way'.

Had it not been for the fact that he had died two years before Hubby, not just died but 'most sincerely died', I would have gone back to the Emerald City and asked the Munchkin Coroner his opinion on the post mortem. It would not have been that tall an order (pun intended) and to be frank (most sincerely frank), it would have been more open-minded than the one with which I have had a brief encounter over recent years. Trust me, he is no Trevor Howard.

Whether the nurses looking after Hubby were employed Eloi or the medics Morlocks, it mattered not, yet they seemed to be living in the same idyllic times on that 'ship' as they did back in 802,701 AD, where they continued to pull together (by and large), walked around in pre-programmed trances (so it often appeared), not mindless necessarily but deliberately marching towards the organisation's litigation authority inside the cave as soon as the clinical negligence siren sounded.

There has seemed little point in taking matters further as there remain two 'hopes' for success, and I do not need to tell you what they are.

Yet I have survived the widowhood effect by four years and nine months to date and protecting the rights of others and the pain I have had to endure whilst slowly dying of a broken heart I hope can eventually be turned into a story that will be of great public interest in which lessons will finally be learned.

All those who work for the ship's Queen continue to sit on their far-from-person-centred thrones. They have been so well-trained as to have me believe that I have actually gone crazy – that I had fallen down that rabbit hole upside down and that all I have claimed happened or should have happened to Hubby has been in my imagination. Raise legitimate concerns or criticisms outside of the 'No Hope Saloon' and one might as well throw oneself overboard before they stick a vexatious label on your big toe or label you as 'unreasonably persistent' on a Twitter feed, if you seek to challenge matters more than once. Even in laughter my heart is in pain. I am trying to remain calm, but I just wanted someone to meet me at the crossroads.

Unlike the Chocolate Factory, where it is claimed that 'nobody ever goes in and nobody ever comes out' (*Charlie and the Chocolate Factory*), nobody ever goes into hospital of their own choosing, but they go in nevertheless, and by and large, most people do come out alive. Bereavement has been the unwelcomed intruder in my life for so long now, and there has been little time to grieve, but bitterness does not go well with my aged complexion. I do not intend to 'draw back that bow and let the poisonous arrows flow straight to all those cold, cold hearts' – no sirree, nor has it been my intention to tar all you medics out there with the same whitewash brush. Sharing my thoughts here has been my own coping strategy for dealing with my grief.

'*Primum non nocere*' – ain't that right doc? That's 'first do no harm' to the likes of you and me. I am far from the 'very merry widow' portrayed in that TV series back in 1969 and if it did not sound so distasteful I could spend my lonely days creating a comparison site. I could call it comparethewidow.com. Hey, maybe that's not a bad idea after all. So I never got to be a virtual assistant but perhaps now I could become a virtual therapist and help others, if based only on my own experience of the complaints system.

'Watch this space', as they say in the editorial business.

Drinking a self-made snowball from a very tall sundae glass, I am saluting the fact that I have not actually gone potty (despite what others might like to think), which feels good, as the clock still has a few more months to go before the hands of 2017 run out. I am not getting sloshed every night and thinking how great it is that I finally get full control of the TV remote, nor grateful for not getting nagged at for putting tramlines in his trousers, but I think I have been more than entitled to have a philosophical moan. I am no longer Mrs Passive, I am now a somewhat Kranky widow who no longer has to worry about putting those dumplings in the stew, and who is getting serious withdrawal symptoms.

These past years have been more than a bumpy ride – a rollercoaster ride in fact, and I have suffered extensive whiplash into the bargain. But I am suffering from battle fatigue right now, and although the MoT on the time machine has run out, I defy anyone to serve me with a statutory notice to quit. I intend to get it up and running again as soon as I can physically and mentally afford to and, God willing, before the mercury starts to take hold.

I have this phenomenal strength of character, you see, which I got from my mum. She too died unexpectedly at the hands of the medical profession just over a year later, and I have to live with the fact that I let her down, because I could not feasibly fight two people's corners at the same time. As Perry Como said, 'It's Impossible'.

And as for Bert, who made up the hat-trick, well, as far as our granddaughter is concerned he has gone to live on a farm. Could be he is running around the fields at Emmerdale with Toto. I like to think so.

PENNY SERENADE

Whether it was the prim and proper dress worn by Sophia Loren in her portrayal of a privileged but bored housewife in *Houseboat*, a 1958 Hollywood movie; the infamous outfit worn by Robin Hood so that he could hide away in Sherwood Forest when attempting to rob from the rich to give to the poor; the short-hooded dress worn by Elizabeth Taylor when marrying Eddie Fisher (husband number four) in 1959; or the reportedly $30,000 dress worn by Scarlett O'Hara in that timeless movie *Gone with the Wind* that I had stolen from her wardrobe one Wednesday afternoon, each of those outfits told their own story in one way or another. One thing they all had in common was the colour green.

Just as the weight of Scarlett's iconic velvet dress is likely to make it come apart at the seams, although I have yet to put it to the test, I have been falling apart at the seams myself ever since I was summoned by the funeral directors to collect my late husband's ashes from the parlour, concealed under a forest green covering. The weight of the world has been resting on my shoulders ever since. It was tailor-made to fit the casket, but no more so than a justice system that has similarly been tailor-made to ensure that those responsible for his death, as I see it, can get away with not having to face the consequences of their actions or inactions that led to my man in the green pyjamas coming home to me in a velvet drawstring bag; a system that has chosen to turn a 'blind' eye.

All those scared little 'mice' – see how they continue to run!

Pardon me if I am a little green with envy therefore that Doris Day's family got to keep her for 95 years (another six and she might have got some egg-roll) and for Olivia De Havilland (aka Melanie, dear Melanie) for making it to the ripe old age of 100 (much to Scarlett's dismay, I am sure), when the person who had been cast as my husband for so long made it to little more than half a century, through no fault of his own.

When you wish upon a star,
Makes no difference who you are
Anything your heart desires will come to you.

If your heart is in your dreams,
No request is too extreme,
When you wish upon a star, as dreamers do.
(*Jiminy Cricket 1940*)

'Makes no difference who you are?' 'No request is too extreme?' If Walt were alive today would he forgive my scepticism, I wonder, if I were to say that the words of the song were little more than philosophical twaddle?

Of course it makes a difference who you are. It's easy coming from someone who had the privilege of owning a lavish £20 million estate with money that could talk in the right places, but I do not begrudge his widow one bit.

And I did not consider my request for a proper investigation into Hubby's death to be that 'extreme', or my expectations that unreasonable, and even if I have been persistent over the years, has it not been my right as his long-standing wife to continue to search for answers as to why we should not be celebrating our ruby wedding anniversary this year but instead remembering the anniversary of his funeral, on that very same day?

Speculations that Mr Disney's body was cryogenically preserved or buried under the Pirates of the Caribbean ride at Disneyland only sought to make light of a sad situation – to make his death sound more glamorous and intriguing when in fact he was cremated and buried at a memorial park like any other normal human being. For years I was convinced he was still alive, only in suspended animation. How easily things can be fabricated. I was not about to let the reputation of the man I loved be tarnished by those who had wronged him so that they could keep their own reputations intact whilst speculating about what might have happened instead of getting down to the nitty gritty.

'Peace and Justice are two sides of the same coin'
Dwight Eisenhower (1890-1969)

'Justice delayed is justice denied'
William Gladstone (1809-1898)

'Charity is no substitute for justice withheld'
Saint Augustine (354-430 AD)

So where are all these guys now, I am thinking, so that I can challenge their philosophies? They have some explaining to do.

Sorry Dwight, but I can have no peace until justice is served, so the ten pence piece that Hubby gave me on our wedding day is still spinning on its axis. Deliberate attempts to delay investigatory matters have been successful, Bill. And working as one of Florence Nightingale's 'disciples' on a full-time basis just to keep my distressed head above water I guess, Your 'Saintship', makes me a charity case.

But a beggar I am not, and it angers me when the 'Wednesbury Principle' is recited to me as a get-out clause for further investigation. What of the Wednesday Principle – the principle being that on this one day I had off mid-week I could travel around the universe in Hollywood style as I had done all those years before; my fun time, with hubby in tow and not a care in the world?

Instead, the happy-go-lucky, romantic and at times, completely bonkers woman you encountered in earlier chapters has since had to spend her time exploring the somewhat controversial relationship between law and medicine. It has not been so much about the controversy surrounding my other half's death but more about the way I have had to handle it. Although he was used to dealing with crime files and I medical files, as previously mentioned, we belonged on the same side of that solitary marital coin.

'Protect and Serve' – except in the clinical world there is no government legislation in place yet that puts medical negligence in the category of a criminal offence in the same way as police law, where the courts settle only for expert medical advice to primarily assist them in determining what 'standards of care' should be. This needs to change.

I have spent so many years fishing for the truth, but I cannot survive the muddy waters for much longer. It is almost time to come up for air. The 'wreck' will come to the surface sooner or later and until it does I shall hold on to the entire 'ship's log' as proof of its existence and the reason for his demise.

My days of crying tears over films like *The Light in the Piazza*, *The Roman Spring of Mrs Stone*, *Who Will Love my Children* and *Random Harvest*, which I used to watch with Mother, are long gone. I have built up this defensive wall, you see, so that I might continue to have the strength and emotional armour to be able to take on all those Pinocchios in da (various) houses when the time comes. They have deprived me of the chance to be the woman I once was. It makes me irritable. I am no longer me.

As Widow Kranky (my new name then - don't wear it out), I am still taking centre stage as the pantomime continues to run. Having worked through almost fifty shades of grey hair dye in my fight for justice so far, my argument has always been that it should not have mattered whether Hubby was a copper or a bin-man, a compulsive drinker or on the wagon, a smoker or non-smoker, I am adamant that the prejudices people face based on lifestyle choices alone should not continue to be repeated or brushed aside due to parliamentary privileges.

If my story were not so long I would write it on a helium balloon, take it out into my garden and let it go as a symbolic release of my pent-up feelings, available for the whole world to read.

On a lighter note, guess who I bumped into the other day in my local Farm Food store.

It was only Sergei, that loveable meerkat. Like him I was looking for a little 'din-din-spiration' as to what I should buy, as I also must continue to eat for one and the butcher had run out of stewing lamb.

We had a heart to heart. I was not looking for a date, but you should see how quickly he ran back to Kovonation Street as if I was trying to 'cop off with him.' No chance. Been there, got the wedding ring. End of. Simples!

Besides, I have a Rhett on standby who may live beyond my own backyard, but I know he will always be there to support and comfort me if only in a cousiny sort of way. Cheers Dave!

Hubby treated me admirably, but in real life he was a Silver Commander – a special kind of 'flutterby' (his childhood name for these winged creatures) – one that cannot be found in any lepidopterist's manual and God willing, in time those responsible for having destroyed his wings will know what they have put me through.

In the meantime, grown up though they are, the kids have written a letter to their daddy, his address is Heaven Above. It says 'Dear Daddy, we miss you and wish you were here with us to love.' Instead of a @ sign they put kisses, Yahoo said that was best to do. They've written this letter to their daddy saying 'we love you.' (Bette Davis, *Whatever Happened to Baby Jane* (1962).

Whatever Happened to Hubby T?
Road to Justice

Now that's two potential films in the making, but first I need to know the ending. I have some hope and Bob Hope. But for now all I can think about is 'back when I was a wife, before this stress removed all my innocence' – if only I could get another chance, another walk, a final glance – how I would love, love, love, to dance with their father again (and my mum and dad for that matter). (Luther Vandross, 2003).

Butterflies may never land on my medical bag on account that I do not have one, but robins have been head-butting my front-door and jumping ferociously on the handles of my patio door from time to time and I am holding on to the thought that this is my Inspector calling on me, as it always seems to be when I am at my lowest.

It has been said that 'when feathers appear, angels are near'. So when a white feather landed on my doorstep only the other day and if, as the Egyptians believe, feathers are a sign of Ma'at – that's the Goddess of Truth, Justice and Order to you and me – then perhaps I will get my wish after all, as I continue to toast his presence every night with a glass of pinot noir.

The doll's house still lies, unopened in the garage – God forbid I must turn it into my own court room just to get heard.

If a picture paints a thousand words, I hope by now that you will at least have a rough sketch of what makes me who I am today and agree that my humour has been honest and touching. In some ways sharing my laughter on paper has been quite healing – written confirmation that Hubby has not been forgotten nor ever will be; the man who used to call elephants 'heffalumps' and would mix up his crocodiles and alligators and come up with a 'crocodilligator' as a child and who, no matter how high up the police ladder he got, continued to receive birthday cards from his mother that started off, 'to ** – mummy's little sod-yer.'

It only leaves me to say then that for the best part I am fine, but every now and then I fall apart. Hey, wasn't that written in a song somewhere?

See you next time, I hope.